GREAT ENDINGS

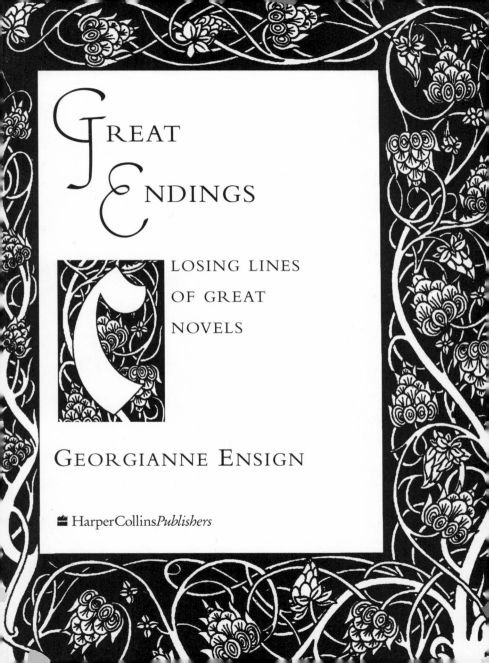

GREAT ENDINGS

CLOSING LINES OF GREAT NOVELS

GEORGIANNE ENSIGN

HarperCollins*Publishers*

Copyright acknowledgments are on page 276.

HarperCollins books may be purchased for educational, business, or sales pro-
motional use. For information please write: Special Markets Department,
HarperCollins Publishers, Inc., 10 East 53rd Street, New York, NY 10022.

FIRST EDITION

Designed by Jessica Shatan

Library of Congress Cataloging-in-Publication Data

Great endings : closing lines of great novels / Georgianne Ensign. — 1st ed.
    p.   cm.
  ISBN 0-06-018347-0 (hc)
    1. Fiction—Technique.   2. Endings (Rhetoric)   3. Quotations, English.
  I. Ensign, Georgianne.
  PN3365.G74   1995
  808.83—dc20   94-46654

95 96 97 98 99 ❖/HC 10 9 8 7 6 5 4 3 2 1

To Richard

Contents ⤵

Acknowledgments ⟿

That this book was a natural sequel to its predecessor, *Great Beginnings: Opening Lines of Great Novels*, was confirmed for me by the number of readers who independently suggested that I write it. I hastened to inform each of them that it had been conceived even before the first book was written, still I would like to thank them all for their votes of confidence.

I am deeply grateful to the staff of the remarkable Kent School John Gray Park Library—where most of the research for this book was conducted—especially Director Marel d'Orbessan Rogers, Judith K. Dike, Lia D. Smits and Leslie S. Snowden; and of the equally surprising Kent Memorial Library and its Head Librarian Deborah Custer, for their enthusiastic help and unfailing consideration.

For their assistance in my research and in extending me permission to publish the wonderful manuscript illustrations in this book, I thank: Jill Faulkner Summers, Stephen J. Joyce and Merlin Holland, for the Estates of William Faulkner, James Joyce and Oscar Wilde, respectively; Patricia C. Willis, Danielle C. McClellan (Beinecke Library, Yale University), C. M. Hall, Alan Marshall, M. Mohamed (The British Library), Kathryn White (The Brontë Society), Leslie A. Morris, Emily C. Walhout (Houghton Library, Harvard University), Jacqueline Cox (King's College Library, Cambridge), Sheila Mortimer (The National Trust), Charles E. Pierce, Jr., Christine Nelson, Kris Elen MacKenzie (Pierpont

Morgan Library), John D. Stinson (Rare Books and Manuscripts Division, New York Public Library), R. Russell Maylone (Northwestern University Library), Dr. William L. Joyce, Margaret M. Sherry, Alice V. Clark (Princeton University Libraries), Una O'Sullivan (Royal Commission on Historical Manuscripts), Anita Goodwin (The Society of Authors), Christine L. Penney (University of Birmingham Library), Alice R. Cotten (University of North Carolina at Chapel Hill), Cathy Henderson, Sally Leach, Diane Goldenberg-Hart (University of Texas at Austin), and Michael Plunkett, Gregory A. Johnson (University of Virginia Library). Also: Alan A. Meyer (Halsey Meyer Higgins), Seán Sweeney (Estate of James Joyce), Fiona Batty (The Peters Fraser & Dunlop Group Ltd.), Edith Golub, Douglass H. G. Gillespie (Macmillan Publishing Company), Owen Laster (William Morris Agency), Linda Shaughnessy (A.P. Watt Ltd.) and Paul Gitlin (Estate of Thomas Wolfe).

Personal thanks are also due Briton Cooper Busch, O. B. Davis, Robin Hulf, Dr. David Kurish, John Leich, my editor, Cynthia Barrett, and my husband, Richard T. Kent.

GREAT ENDINGS

1 ❀ INTRODUCTION

few years ago, there appeared on Broadway a musical with a rather unusual premise: it had no ending. More correctly, it had multiple endings. Because at the conclusion of Act II the audience was invited to choose which of the major characters before them on stage had committed the murder around which the plot revolved.

The musical was *The Mystery of Edwin Drood*, based on Charles Dickens's last novel, and the unique non-ending was necessary because the book itself has no ending; the author had not finished it at the time of his death. Although Dickens left many clues, and his own daughter supported the theory that the murderer was Drood's uncle, John Jasper, Dickens scholars can be no more certain of this solution to the mystery than the Broadway audiences, who often made other choices.

The evening I saw the performance, the audience, which had been restlessly struggling to hear and understand the show's intricate lyrics, became instantly alert as it was offered the opportunity of deciding the ending. And although the "voting" was all in fun, it nevertheless gave the audience a small taste of the responsibility every novelist faces as he or she draws near the last pages of a book: how to end?

Happy or unhappy, hopeful or devastating, the ending brings the story to what is, for the author, the inevitable conclusion. In some respects, ending a story is probably easier than beginning it; conceivably the characters have taken on lives of their own and suggested their own destinies. But ultimately, it is the author who must liberate or kill them, separate or marry them, destroy or save them. And while the author must be true to the characters, he or she must consider the reader as well. For, if a great beginning is vital in capturing a reader's interest, a great ending is equally important in not letting a reader down.

Just as there are many possible ways to begin a story, there are countless ways to end it. In the nascent years of the modern novel, the reader's natural desire for a story to conclude happily for the hero or heroine traditionally led to the type of ending we find in the Austen novels: a marriage, blessed with property and good fortune. In the Victorian and the Edwardian periods, when most novels appeared first in magazine serialization, the importance of satisfying the magazine reader's desire for a happy outcome often resulted in stories with two endings, with the subsequently published book containing the author's preferred, often unhappy, version.

No matter what the outcome, however, the last page of a novel is where loose ends must be tied. In Jane Austen's time, this meant accounting for the future lives of all the major characters in a summary paragraph. In many novels, the last paragraph returns to the opening, like the completion of a circle, echoing the theme, even the title, of the book. Still others paint a last portrait of the hero or heroine having faced the fulfillment or the destruction of his or her life and greeting the future with a new sense of hope. Some endings are so remarkable that the last lines remain in our memory, like poetry. Consider for instance, *Gone with the Wind*: "I'll think of it all tomorrow, at Tara. I can stand it then. Tomorrow, I'll think of some way to get him back. After all, tomorrow is another day." A popular movie and years of parody have made these lines famous, but the desperately brave words of the indomitable Scarlett O'Hara still haunt us from the last page of Margaret Mitchell's classic. They do more than end the story—they leave us satisfied and filled with hope.

Great Endings is a collection of memorable ending lines from great novels, dating from the time of Jane Austen, who more than any other writer shaped the novel as we know it today, to the present. It is not an exhaustive study—what single volume could be?—but it includes selections from much of the world's finest literature, enabling us to examine, compare, and learn from the choices great authors have made. Since it is inevitable that a novelist who began a book brilliantly would end it equally brilliantly, many of the books begun in my collection of opening lines of great novels,

Great Beginnings, will be found ending in this volume. There are many new entries, however, chosen from an endlessly rich variety, including works written both in English and in other languages. For easy comparison, selections are again placed in categories, each of which is introduced by a short discussion of the technique or theme illustrated.

One difference between the two books that immediately comes to mind, of course, is that while a reader needs no previous information to understand a beginning, an ending assumes a good deal of foreknowledge about a novel's characters, plot, and setting. However, I believe that to summarize what has gone before in each novel would have lessened the impact of the bare words and so, in most cases, the passage has been allowed to speak for itself, to be enjoyed and admired as the fine writing it is. Still, where an ending would be totally incomprehensible standing alone, I have prefaced it with a short note.

Like *Great Beginnings*, *Great Endings* offers you the joy of recognizing a favorite work and the thrill of discovering a new one, while it supplies you, if you are a beginning novelist, with a convenient and comprehensive survey of possible options for your own work. Hopefully, reading the ending will not be enough, but will send you back to the book itself, to reread a long-forgotten novel or to open a newly discovered one. The enthusiastic response from those who have enjoyed *Great Beginnings* has suggested to me that there are many closet readers of fiction, some of whom can recite by heart the beginnings of their favorite books. I suspect there are as many who can do the same with endings. And I hope they will find *Great Endings*, alone or as a companion volume to *Great Beginnings*, a natural and useful addition to their libraries as a handy reference, a valuable writer's guide, a comprehensive reading list, and, of course, as pure literary entertainment.

In the end, it is the novelists who have the last word.

2 ❊ Happily Ever After

t is human nature to yearn for happiness. And inevitably our love affair with romance has created generations of disillusioned men and women who were led to believe that marriage was automatically followed by "and they lived happily ever after." Isn't that what always happens in novels?

Reading Jane Austen's *Pride and Prejudice*, we trust from the start that it is only a matter of time before Darcy and Elizabeth find their way to the altar. And a still shorter time before the one obstacle to their happiness, the disapproval of Darcy's aunt, Lady Catherine, is conquered by Elizabeth's patient good nature. All of Jane Austen's novels inevitably end with a marriage or two, "true love, and no want of fortune and friends," and with all of these advantages, it is an understatement to say, as she does in *Northanger Abbey*: "To begin perfect happiness at the respective ages of twenty-six and eighteen is to do pretty well." It's easy to see why we have come to believe that the fulfillment of life is love and marriage, and that in stepping through those portals, we will find the world magically changed from black-and-white to Technicolor, just as it was in *The Wizard of Oz*.

A novel, like a dream, is a never-never land where our fantasies can be indulged and miracles happen. Having entered this other world, we expect that things will end better than they do in our own, and so we will endure any amount of anguish and concern for the hero as long as there is the promise of a light at the end of the story. Every author is well aware of the reader's expectation that all should turn out happily for the hero, and, being in love with his or her own characters, the author probably wishes the same—until those characters persuade him otherwise. There the dilemma arises. Who is to be pleased: the reader or the author?

Experimenting with novel writing in the mid-1800s, Thomas Hardy followed the prescribed formula for happy endings until he had achieved stature enough to end his stories as *he* wished and his characters and the Fates demanded. But even Hardy was forced to alter the manuscript of *Tess of the D'Urbervilles* for magazine serialization, later restoring for the book version language and episodes deemed unfit for the eyes of lady magazine readers. The same ladies, reading the young Rudyard Kipling's novella *The Light That Failed* in the January 1891 *Lippincott's Monthly Magazine*, probably smiled tearfully over the requisite happy but somewhat insipid ending: the blinded artist hero, Dick Heldar, finally engaged to his childhood sweetheart, Maisie, who will selflessly care for him ever after. For this first attempt at novel writing, Kipling had apparently altered the ending on the advice of his American friend and future brother-in-law, the literary agent Wolcott Balestier. But Kipling returned to his original intention in the book version, which contained four additional chapters and a new, unhappy ending: Dick, blind and abandoned by Maisie, his one masterpiece destroyed by the vengeful model Bessie, in one last heroic effort follows his friends to the war in the Sudan, and invites his own death from a bullet to the head. There is no question about which is the better ending, and Kipling knew it.

The Victorians assured us that the hero would live "happily ever after" through a last paragraph or two that glimpsed a perfect future in some detail. This paragraph had the convenience of neatly tying up all the plot's ends and pieces and disposing of those matters that didn't interest the author enough to make them part of the story. Eventually this paragraph was replaced by an entire chapter, the epilogue, which leaped ahead in time to show us what had happened in the years since the end of the story. The epilogue satisfied our curiosity, particularly if the final chapter left the ending in question. Hopefully, its disposition of the characters was not so transparent that the reader would feel betrayed. I myself remember feeling so cheated by the ending to Tom Wolfe's *The Bonfire of the Vanities* that I closed the book (fortunately, a paperback), and threw it across the room. I am not a violent person; my protest was an instinctive reaction against Wolfe's leading me on and then choosing an easy way out, a glib resolution of characters that I felt was intrinsically false.

For, even if the ending is not happy, it must at least seem true.

Of course, a happy ending doesn't always have to take the form of romantic love. Happiness can be the peace that follows conflict, the relief of tension after a rescue, the serenity that comes with self-acceptance, the contentment found in the warmth of the family. "Touched to the heart," reads the end of *Little Women*, "Mrs. March could only stretch out her arms as if to gather children and grandchildren to herself, and say, with face and voice full of motherly love, gratitude, and humility, 'O my girls, however long you may live, I never can wish you a greater happiness than this!'"

With this fervent wish warming our hearts, let us examine some great endings, beginning with the fairy tale "happily ever after."

'Til Death Us Do Part ⌇
The lovers make an eternal vow.

"But don't you want to marry *me?*"

"There's no one else I would marry."

"Then that settles it."

"Mother and Dad will be surprised, won't they?"

"I'm so happy."

"I want my lunch," she said.

"Dear!"

He smiled and took her hand and pressed it. They got up and walked out of the gallery. They stood for a moment at the balustrade and looked at Trafalgar Square. Cabs and omnibuses hurried to and fro, and crowds passed, hastening in every direction, and the sun was shining.

—W. SOMERSET MAUGHAM, *Of Human Bondage*

"Faith," said Coggan, in a critical tone, turning to his companions, "the man hev learnt to say 'my wife' in a wonderful naterel way, considering how very youthful he is in wedlock as yet—hey, neighbours all?"

"I never heerd a skilful old married feller of twenty years' standing pipe 'my wife' in a more used note than 'a did," said Jacob Smallbury. "It might have been a little more true to nater if 't had been spoke a little chillier, but that wasn't to be expected just now."

"That improvement will come wi' time," said Jan, twirling his eye.

Then Oak laughed, and Bathsheba smiled (for she never laughed readily now), and their friends turned to go.

"Yes; I suppose that's the size o't," said Joseph Poorgrass with a cheerful sigh as they moved away; "and I wish him joy o' her; though I were once or twice upon saying to-day with holy Hosea, in my scripture manner, which is my second nature, 'Ephraim is joined to idols: let him alone.' But since 'tis as 'tis, why, it might have been worse, and I feel my thanks accordingly."

—THOMAS HARDY, *Far from the Madding Crowd*

"We must do it as quickly as we can," said Rose. "A consul can marry people. That officer in there spoke about a consul. As soon as we get to the coast . . . "

Allnutt was a little dazed and stupid. This unlooked-for transfer to the West Coast of Africa, this taken-for-granted enlistment in the South African forces, and now this new proposal left him with hardly a word to say. He thought of Rose's moderate superiority in social status. He thought about money; presumably he would receive pay in the South African army. He thought about the girl he had married twelve years ago when he was eighteen. She had probably been through half a dozen men's hands by now, but there had never been a divorce and presumably he was still married to her. Oh well, South Africa and England were a long way apart, and she couldn't trouble him much.

"Righto, Rosie," he said, "let's."

So they left the Lakes and began the long journey to Matadi and marriage. Whether or not they lived happily ever after is not easily decided.

—C. S. FORESTER, *The African Queen*

(Promising it is for the last time, Lord Peter asks Harriet to marry him.)
"Peter!"

She stood still; and he stopped perforce and turned towards her. She laid both hands upon the fronts of his gown, looking into his face while she searched for the word that should carry her over the last difficult breach.

It was he who found it for her. With a gesture of submission he bared his head and stood gravely, the square cap dangling in his hand.

   "Placetne, magistra?"

   "Placet."*

   The Proctor, stumping grimly past with averted eyes, reflected that Oxford was losing all sense of dignity. But what could he do? If Senior Members of the University chose to stand—in their gowns, too!—closely and passionately embracing in New College Lane right under the Warden's windows, he was powerless to prevent it. He primly settled his white bands and went upon his walk unheeded; and no hand plucked his velvet sleeve.

                  —DOROTHY L. SAYERS, *Gaudy Night*

(George Emerson suggests to his new wife, Lucy Honeychurch, that despite all her efforts to keep them apart, her chaperone and cousin, Miss Bartlett, had really meant all along for them to be together.)

". . . Look how she kept me alive in you all the summer; how she gave you no peace; how month after month she became more eccentric and unreliable. The sight of us haunted her—or she couldn't have described us as she did to her friend. There are details—it burnt. I read the book afterwards. She is not frozen, Lucy, she is not withered up all through. She tore us apart twice, but in the Rectory that

---

* *"Does it please the teacher?"*

"It pleases." (trans. John Leich)

evening she was given one more chance to make us happy. We can never make friends with her or thank her. But I do believe that, far down in her heart, far below all speech and behaviour, she is glad."

"It is impossible," murmured Lucy, and then, remembering the experiences of her own heart, she said: "No—it is just possible."

Youth enwrapped them; the song of Phaethon announced passion requited, love attained. But they were conscious of a love more mysterious than this. The song died away; they heard the river, bearing down the snows of winter into the Mediterranean.

—E. M. FORSTER, *A Room With a View*

"O blind André, it was always you—always! Never, never did I think of him, not even for loveless marriage, save once for a little while, when . . . when that theatre girl came into your life, and then . . . " She broke off, shrugged, and turned her head away. "I thought of following ambition, since there was nothing left to follow."

He shook himself. "I am dreaming, of course, or else I am mad," he said.

"Blind, André; just blind," she assured him.

"Blind only where it would have been presumption to have seen."

"And yet," she answered him with a flash of the Aline he had known of old, "I have never found you lack presumption."

M. de Kercadiou, emerging a moment later from the library window, beheld them holding hands and staring each at the other, beatifically, as if each saw Paradise in the other's face.

—RAFAEL SABATINI, *Scaramouche*

"My heart never kissed any other man but you!" she cried. "How often and often and often have I kissed you, and you never knew! . . . It was for a message that I sent George down here—a message to you! . . . I named him after you. . . . Do you think that if dreams could make him your child—he wouldn't be yours—?"

Her courage, and the expression of it, seemed to him to be sublime.

"You don't know me!" she sighed, less convulsively.

"Don't I!" he said with lofty confidence.

After a whole decade his nostrils quivered again to the odour of her olive skin. Drowning amid the waves of her terrible devotion, he was recompensed in the hundredth part of a second for all that through her he had suffered or might hereafter suffer. The many problems and difficulties which marriage with her would raise seemed trivial in the light of her heart's magnificent and furious loyalty. He thought of the younger Edwin whom she had kissed into rapture, as of a boy too inexperienced in sorrow to appreciate this Hilda. He braced himself to the exquisite burden of life.

—ARNOLD BENNETT, *Clayhanger*

(Maggie eases a reconciliation with her Italian prince husband, Amerigo, by speaking kindly of his former lover, her own father's second wife, Charlotte.)

"Isn't she too spendid?" she simply said, offering it to explain and to finish.

"Oh, splendid!" With which he came over to her.

"That's our help, you see," she added—to point further her moral.

It kept him before her therefore, taking in—or trying to—what she so wonderfully gave. He tried, too clearly, to please her—to meet her in her own way; but with the result only that, close to her, her face kept before him, his hands holding her shoulders, his whole act enclosing her, he presently echoed: " 'See'? I see nothing but *you*." And the truth of it had, with this force, after a moment, so strangely lighted his eyes that, as for pity and dread of them, she buried her own in his breast.

—HENRY JAMES, *The Golden Bowl*

"Glad to part again, Estella? To me parting is a painful thing. To me, the remembrance of our last parting has been ever mournful and painful."

"But you said to me," returned Estella, very earnestly, " 'God bless you, God forgive you!' And if you could say that to me then, you will not hesitate to say that to me now—now, when suffering has been stronger than all other teaching, and has taught me to understand what your heart used to be. I have been bent and broken, but—I hope—into a better shape. Be as considerate and good to me as you were, and tell me we are friends."

"We are friends," said I, rising and bending over her, as she rose from the bench.

"And will continue friends apart," said Estella.

I took her hand in mine, and we went out of the ruined place; and, as the morning mists had risen long ago when I first left the forge, so, the evening mists were rising now, and in all the broad expanse of tranquil light they showed to me, I saw no shadow of another parting from her.

—CHARLES DICKENS, *Great Expectations*

(Kester chooses as his wife the narrator of the story, Prudence Sarn, born with a harelip.)

"Tabor on, owd nag!' says Kester, and we were going at a canter towards the blue and purple mountains.

"But no!" I said. "It mun be frommet, Kester. You mun marry a girl like a lily. See, I be hare-shotten!"

But he wouldna listen. He wouldna argufy. Only after I'd pleaded agen myself a long while, he pulled up sharp, and looking down into my eyes, he said—

"No more sad talk! I've chosen my bit of Paradise. 'Tis on your breast, my dear acquaintance!"

And when he'd said those words, he bent his comely head and kissed me full upon the mouth.

. . . . . .

Here ends the story of Prudence Sarn.
—MARY WEBB, *Precious Bane*

Phineas Fogg had won his wager, and had made his journey around the world in eighty days. To do this, he had employed every means of conveyance—steamers, railways, carriages, yachts, trading-vessels, sledges, elephants. The eccentric gentleman had throughout displayed all his marvellous qualities of coolness and exactitude. But what then? What had he really gained by all this trouble? What had he brought back from this long and weary journey?

Nothing, say you? Perhaps so; nothing but a charming woman, who, strange as it may appear, made him the happiest of men!

Truly, would you not for less than that make the tour around the world?

—JULES VERNE, *Around the World in Eighty Days,*
trans. Geo. M. Towle

". . . I think we shall be very happy. I haven't any fears. I think when friends marry, they are safe. We don't suffer like—those young ones," Alexandra ended with a sigh.

They had reached the gate. Before Carl opened it, he drew Alexandra to him and kissed her softly, on her lips and on her eyes.

She leaned heavily on his shoulder. "I am tired," she murmured. "I have been very lonely, Carl."

They went into the house together, leaving the Divide behind them, under the evening star. Fortunate country, that is one day to receive hearts like Alexandra's into its bosom, to give them out again in the yellow wheat, in the rustling corn, in the shining eyes of youth!

—WILLA CATHER, *O Pioneers!*

"If you come with me it will be a hard life, and a wild one at times, Mary, with no biding anywhere, and little rest and comfort. Men are ill companions when the mood takes them, and I, God knows, the worst of them. You'll get a poor exchange for your farm, and small prospect of the peace you crave."

"I'll take the risk, Jem, and chance your moods."

"Do you love me, Mary?"

"I believe so, Jem."

"Better than Helford?"

"I can't ever answer that."

"Why are you sitting here beside me, then?"

"Because I want to; because I must; because now and for evermore this is where I belong to be," said Mary.

He laughed then and took her hand and gave her the reins; and she did not look back over her shoulder again, but set her face towards the Tamar.

—DAPHNE DU MAURIER, *Jamaica Inn*

. . . Pearl lay, thinking her own thoughts, looking up at the big prairie stars which hung so lone and coldly overhead. Pearl spread her blankets. She hardly felt as if she'd slept at all when she began to dream that she was in the immigrant train and the men's heels were kicking on the tin roof of the car; the train was rocking, falling off the track. She opened her eyes, terrified, and found it was daylight and a man was beside her, shaking her lightly by the shoulder.

"Jesse!" Pearl cried. Still half-confused by sleep she sat up, trying to put her arms around his neck. But Jesse pulled back.

"What kind of a wife stays in bed all day, the first day out?"

"The same kind whose husband stays out all night, his wedding night."

"We can fix that," Jesse said calmly. Grinning at her, he sat down beside the bed-roll and began to take his boots off.

—NIVEN BUSCH, *Duel in the Sun*

The taxi passed Macon's hotel—brown and tidy, strangely homelike. A man was just emerging with a small anxious dog on his arm. And there on the curb stood Muriel, surrounded by suitcases and string-handled shopping bags and cardboard cartons overflowing with red velvet. She was frantically waving down taxis—first one ahead, then Macon's own. *"Arrêtez!"* Macon cried to the driver. The taxi lurched to a halt. A sudden flash of sunlight hit the windshield, and spangles flew across the glass. The spangles were old water spots, or maybe the markings of leaves, but for a moment Macon thought they were something else. They were so bright and festive, for a moment he thought they were confetti.

—ANNE TYLER, *The Accidental Tourist*

(From Molly Bloom's soliloquy)

. . . and the wineshops half open at night and the castanets and the night we missed the boat at Algeciras the watchman going about serene with his lamp and O that awful deep-down torrent O and the sea the sea crimson sometimes like fire and the glorious sunsets and the figtrees in the Alameda gardens yes and all the queer little streets and pink and blue and yellow houses and the rosegardens and the jessamine and geraniums and cactuses and Gibraltar as a girl where I was a Flower of the mountain yes when I put the rose in my hair like the Andalusian girls used or shall I wear a red yes and how he kissed me under the Moorish wall and I thought well as well him as another and then I asked him with my eyes to ask again yes and then he asked me would I yes to say yes my mountain flower and first I put my arms around him yes and drew him down to me so he could feel my breasts all perfume yes and his heart was going like mad and yes I said yes I will Yes.

—JAMES JOYCE, *Ulysses*

Future Perfect ✍
A view into the crystal ball.

Lady Catherine was extremely indignant on the marriage of her nephew; and as she gave way to all the genuine frankness of her character, in her reply to the letter which announced its arrangement, she sent him language so very abusive, especially of Elizabeth, that for some time all intercourse was at

The first page of a letter from James Joyce to Robert McAlmon, October 29, 1921, describing the completion of *Ulysses:* "at last the writing of *Ulysses* is finished. I have still a lot of proofchecking and revising to do but the composition is at an end." *(Yale Collection of American Literature, Beinecke Rare Book and Manuscript Library, Yale University)* an end. But at length, by Elizabeth's persuasion, he was prevailed on to overlook the offence, and seek a reconciliation; and, after a little further resistance on the part of his aunt, her resentment gave way, either to her affection for him, or her curiosity to see how his wife conducted herself: and she condescended to wait on them at Pemberley, in spite of that pollution which its woods had received, not merely from the presence of such a mistress, but the visits of her uncle and aunt from the city.

With the Gardiners they were always on the most intimate terms. Darcy, as well as Elizabeth, really loved them; and they were both ever sensible of the warmest gratitude towards the persons who, by bringing her into Derbyshire, had been the means of uniting them.

—JANE AUSTEN, *Pride and Prejudice*

Mrs. Dashwood was prudent enough to remain at the cottage, without attempting a removal to Delaford; and fortunately for Sir John and Mrs. Jennings, when Marianne was taken from them, Margaret had reached an age highly suitable for dancing, and not very ineligible for being supposed to have a lover.

Between Barton and Delaford, there was that constant communication which strong family affection would naturally dictate; and among the merits and the happiness of Elinor and Marianne, let it not be ranked as the least considerable, that though sisters, and living almost within sight of each other, they could live without disagreement between themselves, or producing coolness between their husbands.

—JANE AUSTEN, *Sense and Sensibility*

The result of this distress, was, that, with a much more voluntary, cheerful consent than his daughter had ever presumed to hope for at the moment, she was able to fix her wedding-day; and Mr. Elton was called on, within a month from the marriage of Mr. and Mrs. Robert Martin, to join the hands of Mr. Knightley and Miss Woodhouse.

The wedding was very much like other weddings, where the parties have no taste for finery or parade; and Mrs. Elton, from the particulars detailed by her husband, thought it all extremely shabby, and very inferior to her own. "Very little white satin, very few lace veils; a most pitiful business! Selina would stare when she heard of it." But, in spite of these deficiencies, the wishes, the hopes, the confidence, the predictions of the small band of true friends who witnessed the ceremony, were fully answered in the perfect happiness of the union.

—JANE AUSTEN, *Emma*

Elizabeth accepted him gladly. He was rather old, perhaps, but a Deputy Commissioner is not to be despised—certainly he was a far better match than Flory. They are very happy. Mr. Macgregor was always a good-hearted man, but he has grown more human and likeable since his marriage. His voice booms less, and he has given up his morning exercises. Elizabeth has grown mature surprisingly quickly, and a certain hardness of manner that always belonged to her has become accentuated. Her servants live in terror of her, though she speaks no Burmese. She has an exhaustive knowledge of the Civil List, gives charming little dinner-parties and knows how to put the wives of subordinate officials in their places—in short, she fills with complete success the position for which Nature had designed her from the first, that of a burra memsahib.

—GEORGE ORWELL, *Burmese Days*

(Eugénie Grandet, who had paid the debts of her unfaithful fiancé so that he could marry a nobleman's daughter, is left a wealthy widow though a marriage of convenience to one of her old suitors. She lives on in great wealth with the family servant, Nanon, and the servant's husband.)

"No one loves me but you," she would sometimes say to Nanon.

Yet her hands are always ready to bind the wounds that other eyes do not see, in any house; and her way to heaven is one long succession of kindness and good deeds. The real greatness of her soul has risen above the cramping influences of her early life. And this is the life history of a woman who dwells in the world, yet is not of it, a woman so grandly fitted to be a wife and mother, but who has neither husband nor children nor kindred.

Of late the good folk of Saumur have begun to talk of a

second marriage for her. Rumor is busy with her name and that of the Marquis de Froidfond; indeed, his family have begun to surround the rich widow, just as the Cruchots once flocked about Eugénie Grandet. Nanon and Cornoiller, so it is said, are in the interest of the Marquis, but nothing could be more false; for big Nanon and Cornoiller have neither of them wit enough to understand the corruptions of the world.

—HONORÉ DE BALZAC, *Eugénie Grandet*

As you look at Wendy you may see her hair becoming white, and her figure little again, for all this happened long ago. Jane is now a common grown-up, with a daughter called Margaret; and every spring-cleaning time, except when he forgets, Peter comes for Margaret and takes her to the Neverland, where she tells him stories about himself, to which he listens eagerly. When Margaret grows up she will have a daughter, who is to be Peter's mother in turn; and so it will go on, so long as children are gay and innocent and heartless.

—J. M. BARRIE, *Peter and Wendy*

(Jane Eyre, after fleeing from Thornfield, is rescued by the Reverend St. John Rivers and his sisters, who are revealed to be her cousins. Before Jane can decline Rivers's proposal of marriage, a dream calls her back to a blinded Mr. Rochester; in her happiness with him, she reflects on the minister's fate.)

St. John is unmarried: he never will marry now. Himself has hitherto sufficed to the toil; and the toil draws near its close:

his glorious sun hastens to its setting. The last letter I
received from him drew from my eyes human tears, and yet
filled my heart with Divine joy: he anticipated his sure
reward, his incorruptible crown. I know that a stranger's
hand will write to me next, to say that the good and faithful
servant has been called at length into the joy of his Lord.
And why weep for this? No fear of death will darken St.
John's last hour: his mind will be unclouded; his heart will be
undaunted; his hope will be sure; his faith steadfast. His own
words are a pledge of this:—

"My Master," he says, "has forewarned me. Daily he
announces more distinctly,—'Surely I come quickly!' and
hourly I more eagerly respond,—'Amen; even so come, Lord
Jesus!' "

—CHARLOTTE BRONTË, *Jane Eyre*

. . . Mr. Pickwick is somewhat infirm now; but he retains
all his former juvenility of spirit, and may still be frequently
seen, contemplating the pictures in the Dulwich Gallery, or
enjoying a walk about the pleasant neighbourhood on a fine
day. He is known by all the poor people about, who never
fail to take their hats off, as he passes, with great respect; the
children idolize him; and so indeed does the whole
neighbourhood. Every year, he repairs to a large family
merry-making at Mr. Wardle's; on this, as on all other
occasions, he is invariably attended by the faithful Sam,
between whom and his master there exists a steady

hill; a more resolute, indefatigable pioneer never wrought amidst rocks and dangers. Firm, faithful and devoted, full of energy and zeal and truth, he labours for his race; he clears their painful way to improvement; he hews down like a giant the prejudices of creed and caste that encumber it. He may be stern, he may be exacting, he may be ambitious yet, but his is the sternness of the warrior Great-heart who guards his pilgrim-convoy from the onslaught of Apollyon; his is the exaction of the apostle who speaks but for Christ when he says: "Whosoever will come after me, let him deny himself and take up his cross and follow me;" his is the ambition of the high master-spirit which aims to fill a place in the first rank of those who are redeemed from the earth, who stand without fault before the throne of God, who share the last mighty victories of the Lamb, who are called and chosen and faithful.

St. John is unmarried; he never will marry now, himself has hitherto sufficed to the toil and the toil draws near its close; his glorious sun hastens to its setting. The last letter I received from him drew from my eyes human tears and yet filled my heart with divine joy: he anticipated his sure reward, his incorruptible crown: I know that a stranger's hand will write to me next to say that the good and faithful servant has been called at length into the joy of his Lord. And why weep for this? No fear of death will darken St. John's last hour; his mind will be unclouded, his heart will be undaunted, his hope will be sure, his faith steadfast. His own words are a pledge of this:

"My Master" he says "has forewarned me; daily he announces more distinctly 'Surely I come quickly'; and hourly I more eagerly respond 'Amen; even so come, Lord Jesus!' "

Finis

19th   1847

The last page of the original manuscript of Charlotte Brontë's *Jane Eyre. (The British Library, Add. 43, 476-f. 265)* and reciprocal attachment, which nothing but death will terminate.

—CHARLES DICKENS, *The Posthumous Papers of the Pickwick Club*

Tom's most well now, and got his bullet around his neck on a watch-guard for a watch, and is always seeing what time it is, and so there ain't nothing more to write about, and I am rotten glad of it, because if I'd 'a' knowed what a trouble it was to make a book I wouldn't 'a' tackled it, and ain't a-going to no more. But I reckon I got to light out for the territory ahead of the rest, because Aunt Sally she's going to adopt me and sivilize me, and I can't stand it. I been there before.

—MARK TWAIN, *The Adventures of Huckleberry Finn*

. . . When the thieves prevailed at length, as they did, forcing cattle owners to leave the country or be ruined, the Virginian had forestalled this crash. The herds were driven away to Montana. Then, in 1892, came the cattle war, when, after putting their men in office, and coming to own some of the newspapers, the thieves brought ruin on themselves as well. For in a broken country there is nothing left to steal.

But the railroad came, and built a branch to that land of the Virginian's where the coal was. By that time he was an important man, with a strong grip on many various enterprises, and able to give his wife all and more than she asked or desired. Sometimes she missed the Bear Creek days, when she and he had ridden together, and sometimes she declared that his work would kill him. But it does not seem to have done so. Their eldest boy rides the horse Monte; and, strictly between ourselves, I think his father is going to live a long while.

—OWEN WISTER, *The Virginian*

Future Almost Perfect ↶
Happiness of a sort.

(About two years after Quasimodo's mysterious disappearance and the execution of Esmeralda, in the cave of Montfaucon, where the bodies of the guilty and innocent were thrown. . .)

. . . there were found amongst all those hideous carcases two skeletons, the arms of one of which were thrown round the other. One of the two, that of a woman, had still about it some tattered fragments of a garment, apparently of a stuff that had once been white; and about its neck was a string of grains of adrezarach, together with a small silken bag, ornamented with green glass, which was open and empty. These articles had been of so little value that the executioner, doubtless, had not cared to take them. The other skeleton, which held this one close in its arms, was that of a man. It was remarked in the latter that the spine was crooked, the head compressed between the shoulder-blades, and that one leg was shorter than the other. It was also remarkable that there was no rupture of the vertebræ at the nape of the neck, whence it was evident that he had not been hanged. Hence

it was inferred that the man must have come hither of himself and died here. When they strove to detach this skeleton
from the one it was embracing, it fell to dust.

—VICTOR HUGO, *Notre-Dame de Paris*

Yeobright had, in fact, found his vocation in the career of an
itinerant open-air preacher and lecturer on morally unim-
peachable subjects; and from this day he laboured incessantly
in that office, speaking not only in simple language on Rain-
barrow and in the hamlets round, but in a more cultivated
strain elsewhere—from the steps and porticoes of town-halls,
from market-crosses, from conduits, on esplanades and on
wharves, from the parapets of bridges, in barns and out-
houses, and all other such places in the neighbouring Wessex
towns and villages. He left alone creeds and systems of philosophy, finding enough and more than enough to occupy
his tongue in the opinions and actions common to all good
men. Some believed him, and some believed not; some said
that his words were commonplace, others complained of his
want of theological doctrine; while others again remarked that
it was well enough for a man to take to preaching who could
not see to do anything else. But everywhere he was kindly
received, for the story of his life had become generally known.

—THOMAS HARDY, *The Return of the Native*

The same fate attended Judith. When Hawkeye reached the
garrison on the Mohawk, he inquired anxiously after that

lovely, but misguided creature. None knew her—even her person was no longer remembered. Other officers had again and again succeeded the Warleys and Craigs and Grahams; though an old sergeant of the garrison, who had lately come from England, was enabled to tell our hero that Sir Robert Warley lived on his paternal estates, and that there was a lady of rare beauty in the lodge, who had great influence over him, though she did not bear his name. Whether this was Judith, relapsed into her early failing, or some other victim of the soldier's, Hawkeye never knew, nor would it be pleasant or profitable to inquire. We live in a world of transgressions and selfishness, and no pictures that represent us otherwise can be true; though happily for human nature, gleamings of that pure spirit in whose likeness man has been fashioned, are to be seen, relieving its deformities, and mitigating, if not excusing its crimes.

—JAMES FENIMORE COOPER, *The Deerslayer*

To the Rescue ⌒

The danger is over, and the hero safe and sound.

(Sir Percy is secretly the leader of the League of the Scarlet Pimpernel, a band of Englishmen who rescue victims from the Reign of Terror in Paris, and particularly from M. Chauvelin.)

The rest is silence!—silence and joy for those who had endured so much suffering, yet found at last a great and lasting happiness.

But it is on record that at the brilliant wedding of Sir

Andrew Ffoulkes, Bart., with Mlle. Suzanne de Tournay de Basserive, a function at which H.R.H. the Prince of Wales and all the *élite* of fashionable society were present, the most beautiful woman there was unquestionably Lady Blakeney, whilst the clothes Sir Percy Blakeney wore were the talk of the *jeunesse dorée* of London for many days.

It is also a fact that M. Chauvelin, the accredited agent of the French Republican Government, was not present at that or any other social function in London, after that memorable evening at Lord Grenville's ball.

—BARONESS ORCZY, *The Scarlet Pimpernel*

None the less, he knew that the tale he had to tell could not be one of a final victory. It could be only the record of what had had to be done, and what assuredly would have to be done again in the never ending fight against terror and its relentless onslaughts, despite their personal afflictions, by all who, while unable to be saints but refusing to bow down to pestilences, strive their utmost to be healers.

And, indeed, as he listened to the cries of joy rising from the town, Rieux remembered that such joy is always imperiled. He knew what those jubilant crowds did not know but could have learned from books: that the plague bacillus never dies or disappears for good; that it can lie dormant for years and years in furniture and linen-chests; that it bides its time in bedrooms, cellars, trunks, and bookshelves; and that perhaps the day would come when, for the bane and the enlightening of men, it would rouse up its rats again and send them forth to die in a happy city.

—ALBERT CAMUS, *The Plague,* trans. Stuart Gilbert

(The schoolboys, with their leader, Ralph, are found on the desert island on which they had struggled to survive after an airplane crash.) Ralph looked at him dumbly. For a moment he had a fleeting picture of the strange glamour that had once invested the beaches. But the island was scorched up like dead wood—Simon was dead—and Jack had. . . . The tears began to flow and sobs shook him. He gave himself up to them now for the first time on the island; great, shuddering spasms of grief that seemed to wrench his whole body. His voice rose under the black smoke before the burning wreckage of the island; and infected by that emotion, the other little boys began to shake and sob too. And in the middle of them, with filthy body, matted hair, and unwiped nose, Ralph wept for the end of innocence, the darkness of man's heart, and the fall through the air of the true, wise friend called Piggy.

The officer, surrounded by these noises, was moved and a little embarrassed. He turned away to give them time to pull themselves together; and waited, allowing his eyes to rest on the trim cruiser in the distance.

—WILLIAM GOLDING, *Lord of the Flies*

Aunt Em had just come out of the house to water the cabbages when she looked up and saw Dorothy running toward her.

"My darling child!" she cried, folding the little girl in her arms and covering her face with kisses, "where in the world did you come from?"

"From the Land of Oz," said Dorothy gravely. "And here is Toto, too. And oh, Aunt Em! I'm so glad to be at home again!"

—L. FRANK BAUM, *The Wizard of Oz*

The papers carried the story. "Chain saw balks bizarre homicide. Eliot Nailles, of Chestnut Lane, Bullet Park, New York, cut his way through the locked door of Christ's Church early last evening with a chain saw and succeeded in saving the life of his son, Anthony. Paul Hammer, also of Bullet Park, confessed to attempted homicide and was remanded to the State Hospital for the Criminally Insane. Hammer confessed to having kidnapped the young man from a dinner party given by Mr. and Mrs. Thomas Lewellen of Marlborough Circle. He carried Nailles to the church with the object of immolating him in the chancel. He intended, he claimed, to awaken the world."

Tony went back to school on Monday and Nailles—drugged—went off to work and everything was as wonderful, wonderful, wonderful, wonderful as it had been.

—JOHN CHEEVER, *Bullet Park*

(Pursued by the Elder, Tull, for befriending Gentiles, Mormon rancher Jane Withersteen escapes with the gun-man, Lassiter, through a cliff divide with an overhanging rock.)

"Roll the stone! . . . Lassiter, I love you!"

Under all his deathly pallor, and the blood, and the iron of seared cheek and lined brow, worked a great change. He placed both hands on the rock and then leaned his shoulder there and braced his powerful body.

"ROLL THE STONE!"

It stirred, it groaned, it grated, it moved; and with a slow grinding, as of wrathful relief, began to lean. It had waited ages to fall, and now was slow in starting. Then, as if suddenly instinct with life, it leaped hurtlingly down to alight on the steep incline, to bound more swiftly into the air, to gather momentum, to plunge into the lofty leaning crag below. The crag thundered into atoms. A wave of air—a splitting shock! Dust shrouded the sunset red of shaking rims; dust shrouded Tull as he fell on his knees with uplifted arms. Shafts and monuments and sections of wall fell majestically.

From the depths there rose a long-drawn rumbling roar. The outlet to Deception Pass closed forever.

—ZANE GREY, *Riders of the Purple Sage*

(With no money for food, Ma Joad asks her daughter, who has just delivered a stillborn child, to save a sick and starving young man they find in a sheltering barn.)

For a minute Rose of Sharon sat still in the whispering barn. Then she hoisted her tired body up and drew the comfort about her. She moved slowly to the corner and stood looking down at the wasted face, into the wide, frightened eyes.

Then slowly she lay down beside him. He shook his head slowly from side to side. Rose of Sharon loosened one side of the blanket and bared her breast. "You got to," she said. She squirmed closer and pulled his head close. "There!" she said. "There." Her hand moved behind his head and supported it. Her fingers moved gently in his hair. She looked up and across the barn, and her lips came together and smiled mysteriously.

—JOHN STEINBECK, *The Grapes of Wrath*

Brody put his face into the water and opened his eyes. Through the stinging saltwater mist he saw the fish sink in a slow and graceful spiral, trailing behind it the body of Quint—arms out to the sides, head thrown back, mouth open in mute protest.

The fish faded from view. But, kept from sinking into the deep by the bobbing barrels, it stopped somewhere beyond the reach of light, and Quint's body hung suspended, a shadow twirling slowly in the twilight.

Brody watched until his lungs ached for air. He raised his head, cleared his eyes, and sighted in the distance the black point of the water tower. Then he began to kick toward shore.

—PETER BENCHLEY, *Jaws*

(Humphrey Van Weyden and the poet Maude Brewster are rescued from a desert island and the ruthless captain of the schooner Ghost.*)*

Her lips met the press of mine, and, by what strange trick of the imagination I know not, the scene in the cabin of the *Ghost* flashed upon me, when she had pressed her fingers lightly on my lips and said, "Hush, hush."

"My woman, my one small woman," I said, my free hand petting her shoulder in the way all lovers know though never learn in school.

"My man," she said, looking at me for an instant with tremulous lids which fluttered down and veiled her eyes as she snuggled her head against my breast with a happy little sigh.

I looked toward the cutter. It was very close. A boat was being lowered.

"One kiss, dear love," I whispered. "One kiss more before they come."

"And rescue us from ourselves," she completed, with a most adorable smile, whimsical as I had never seen it, for it was whimsical with love.

—JACK LONDON, *The Sea-Wolf*

(The ship arrives in Germany from Mexico in 1931 with its motley collection of passengers after a twenty-seven-day voyage and a man overboard.)
The band played "Tannenbaum" at last, and kept it up until the gangplank was down, and the passengers began to descend rapidly and silently. As the musicians were wiping the mouthpieces of their instruments, wrapping up their drums and putting away their fiddles, their mouths were

wide with smiles, their heads towards the dock, towards the exact narrow spot where the *Vera* had warped in and cast her anchor. Among them, a gangling young boy, who looked as if he had never had enough to eat in his life, nor a kind word from anybody, and did not know what he was going to do next, stared with blinded eyes, his mouth quivering while he shook the spit out of his trumpet, repeating to himself just above a whisper, *"Grüss Gott, Grüss Gott,"* as if the town were a human being, a good and dear trusted friend who had come a long way to welcome him.

—KATHERINE ANNE PORTER, *Ship of Fools*

And somewhere in there was springtime. The corpse mines were closed down. The soldiers all left to fight the Russians. In the suburbs, the women and children dug rifle pits. Billy and the rest of his group were locked up in the stable in the suburbs. And then, one morning, they got up to discover that the door was unlocked. World War Two in Europe was over.

Billy and the rest wandered out onto the shady street. The trees were leafing out. There was nothing going on out there, no traffic of any kind. There was only one vehicle, an abandoned wagon drawn by two horses. The wagon was green and coffin-shaped.

Birds were talking.

One bird said to Billy Pilgrim, *"Poo-tee-weet?"*

—KURT VONNEGUT, JR., *Slaughterhouse-Five*

Triumph ⌐⌐

Great and small successes of the spirit.

Quickly, as if she were recalled by something over there, she
turned to her canvas. There it was—her picture. Yes, with all
its greens and blues, its lines running up and across, its
attempt at something. It would be hung in the attics, she
thought; it would be destroyed. But what did that matter?
she asked herself, taking up her brush again. She looked at
the steps; they were empty; she looked at her canvas; it was
blurred. With a sudden intensity, as if she saw it clear for a
second, she drew a line there, in the centre. It was done; it
was finished. Yes, she thought, laying down her brush in
extreme fatigue, I have had my vision.

—VIRGINIA WOOLF, *To the Lighthouse*

(In this imagined "prequel" to Charlotte Brontë's Jane Eyre, *Mr.
Rochester's demented wife escapes from her keeper in the attic of Thornfield Hall to light the fire that will destroy it and blind him.)*
Grace Poole was sitting at the table but she had heard the
scream too, for she said, "What was that?" She got up, came
over and looked at me. I lay still, breathing evenly with my
eyes shut. "I must have been dreaming," she said. Then she
went back, not to the table but to her bed. I waited a long
time after I heard her snore, then I got up, took the keys and
unlocked the door. I was outside holding my candle. Now at
last I know why I was brought here and what I have to do.

There must have been a draught for the flame flickered and I thought it was out. But I shielded it with my hand and it burned up again to light me along the dark passage.

—JEAN RHYS, *Wide Sargasso Sea*

(After the death of Dr. Juvenal Urbino fifty years after their marriage, his widow, Fermina Daza, is reunited with Florentino Ariza, whose love she had spurned for Urbino's position and wealth. On a riverboat trip, they finally consummate their love.)
The Captain looked at Fermina Daza and saw on her eyelashes the first glimmer of wintry frost. Then he looked at Florentino Ariza, his invincible power, his intrepid love, and he was overwhelmed by the belated suspicion that it is life, more than death, that has no limits.

"And how long do you think we can keep up this goddamn coming and going?" he asked.

Florentino Ariza had kept his answer ready for fifty-three years, seven months, and eleven days and nights.

"Forever," he said.

—GABRIEL GARCÍA MÁRQUEZ, *Love in the Time of Cholera*,
trans. Edith Grossman

(Lashed to the old fisherman's boat are the remains of the great marlin he has caught, which was ravaged by sharks as he returned from the sea.)
That afternoon there was a party of tourists at the Terrace and looking down in the water among the empty beer cans and dead barracudas a woman saw a great long white spine

with a huge tail at the end that lifted and swung with the tide while the east wind blew a heavy steady sea outside the entrance to the harbour.

"What's that?" she asked a waiter and pointed to the long backbone of the great fish that was now just garbage waiting to go out with the tide.

"Tiburon," the waiter said, "Eshark." He was meaning to explain what had happened.

"I didn't know sharks had such handsome, beautifully formed tails."

"I didn't either," her male companion said.

Up the road, in his shack, the old man was sleeping again. He was still sleeping on his face and the boy was sitting by him watching him. The old man was dreaming about the lions.

—ERNEST HEMINGWAY, *The Old Man and the Sea*

But he is not always alone. When the long winter nights come on and the wolves follow their meat into the lower valleys, he may be seen running at the head of the pack through the pale moonlight or glimmering borealis, leaping gigantic above his fellows, his great throat a-bellow as he sings a song of the younger world, which is the song of the pack.

—JACK LONDON, *The Call of the Wild*

(The blinded Dick Heldar seeks death in the desert.)
"Get down, man! Get down behind the camel!"

"No. Put me, I pray, in the forefront of the battle." Dick turned his face to Torpenhow and raised his hand to set his helmet straight, but, miscalculating the distance, knocked it off. Torpenhow saw that his hair was grey on the temples, and that his face was the face of an old man.

"Come down, you damned fool! Dickie, come off!"

And Dick came obediently, but as a tree falls, pitching sideways from the Bisharin's saddle at Torpenhow's feet. His luck had held to the last, even to the crowning mercy of a kindly bullet through his head.

Torpenhow knelt under the lee of the camel, with Dick's body in his arms.

—RUDYARD KIPLING, *The Light That Failed*

(Stalked by his former friend, Guitar, Milkman jumps from the outcropping called Solomon's Leap—and flies.)

Squatting on the edge of the other flat-headed rock with only the night to cover him, Guitar smiled over the barrel of his rifle. "My man," he murmured to himself. "My main man." He put the rifle on the ground and stood up.

Milkman stopped waving and narrowed his eyes. He could just make out Guitar's head and shoulders in the dark. "You want my life?" Milkman was not shouting now. "You need it? Here." Without wiping away the tears, taking a deep breath, or even bending his knees—he leaped. As fleet and bright as a lodestar he wheeled toward Guitar and it did not matter which one of them would give up his ghost in the killing arms of his brother. For now he knew

Detail from the original manuscript of the "happy ending" version of Rudyard Kipling's *The Light That Failed*, written for the January 1891 *Lippincott's Monthly Magazine* and later changed to the unhappy ending Kipling preferred in the book version. *(Frank N. Doubleday and Nelson Doubleday Collection, Manuscripts Division, Department of Rare Books and Special Collections, Princeton University Libraries)* what Shalimar knew: If you surrendered to the air, you could *ride* it.

—TONI MORRISON, *Song of Solomon*

(Movie director Harold Heston has filmed the near suicidal stunt leap of his father, Dan Prader, on horseback, from a cliff into the sea.)
Night fell on the cliffs above the sea; the tough grass, filling with moisture, straightened where the wheels of the vehicles had mashed it down. All equipment used that day, including the wood from Dan's chute, had been removed when the company left. Soon there would be little proof that human beings had ever been there, except a piece of film showing a man and horse jumping from the cliffs into the sea—even this in a fashion would always be questionable, man and horse in the film being only shadows or dream-shapes and hence not proof of anything in the real world.

—NIVEN BUSCH, *The Actor*

(Bob Slocum overcomes his fears and loss of confidence and takes control of his life just as, at the office, Martha the typist goes crazy.)
We have a good-sized audience now, and I am the supervisor. Martha rises compliantly, smiling, with a hint of diabolical satisfaction, I see, at the wary attention she has succeeded in extorting from so many people who are solicitous and alarmed.

   "There, there, dear."

"Come along, dear."

"That's nice, dear."

"Take your purse, dear. And your book."

"Do you want to rest, dear?"

"Do you have a roommate, dear? Someone we can call?"

"Would you like to lie down, dear? While we're waiting for the car?"

"That's fine, dear."

"Good-bye, Martha."

"Good-bye, Martha dear."

"Bye, bye, dear."

"Did you leave anything behind?"

"Don't worry, dear. We'll send it along."

"Be gentle with her," I adjure. "She's a wonderful girl."

I hear applause when she's gone for the way I handled it. No one was embarrassed.

Everyone seems pleased with the way I've taken command.

—JOSEPH HELLER, *Something Happened*

Home Sweet Home ↬
The cat's on the hearth and all is peace at last.

(The novel ends as it began, with a Letter to God.)

I feel a little peculiar round the children. For one thing, they grown. And I see they think me and Nettie and Shug and Albert and Samuel and Harpo and Sofia and Jack and Odessa real old and don't know much what going on. But I don't

think us feel old at all. And us so happy. Matter of fact, I
think this the youngest us ever felt.

Amen

—ALICE WALKER, *The Color Purple*

*(The Italian mistress of the late poet, Howard Beaver, awaits the arrival
of the young woman who may be editing his letters.)*
The old woman smiles and nods to herself. A blue butterfly
settles on her folded spectacles. Life is still pleasant. She has
wit and power and she owns beauty. The white peacocks
strut and flaunt. The scent of lavender fills the evening air,
blending with the blue smoke of the little cigar. She is filled
with pleasurable anticipation as she hears the wheels of the
hired Renault crunch along the gravel drive.

—MARGARET DRABBLE, *A Natural Curiosity*

(Ethel Cobbett has been fired from the Literary World *by its editor,
Burlap.)*
Thank goodness, he reflected, as he walked along whistling
"On Wings of Song" with rich expression, that was the end
of Ethel Cobbett so far as he was concerned. It was the end
of her also as far as everybody was concerned. For some few
days later, having written him a twelve-page letter, which he
put in the fire after reading the first scarifying sentence, she
lay down with her head in an oven and turned on the gas.
But that was something which Burlap could not foresee. His
mood as he walked whistling homeward was one of unmixed

contentment. That night he and Beatrice pretended to be two little children and had their bath together. Two little children sitting at opposite ends of the big old-fashioned bath. And what a romp they had! The bathroom was drenched with their splashings. Of such is the Kingdom of Heaven.

—ALDOUS HUXLEY, *Point Counter Point*

He stopped on the threshold, startled; for, from the waxen face on the pillow, almost it seemed the eyes of Isabel herself were looking at him: never before had the resemblance between mother and son been so strong—and Eugene knew that now he had once seen it thus startlingly, he need divest himself of no bitterness "to be kind" to Georgie.

George was startled, too. He lifted a white hand in a queer gesture, half forbidding, half imploring, and then let his arm fall back upon the coverlet. "You must have thought my mother wanted you to come," he said, "so that I could ask you to—to forgive me."

But Lucy, who sat beside him, lifted ineffable eyes from him to her father, and shook her head. "No, just to take his hand—gently!"

She was radiant.

But for Eugene another radiance filled the room. He knew that he had been true at last to his true love, and that through him she had brought her boy under shelter again. Her eyes would look wistful no more.

—BOOTH TARKINGTON, *The Magnificent Ambersons*

(Margaret asks her husband if it is true that his dead first wife had left the cottage, Howard's End, to her.)

Tranquilly he replied: "Yes, she did. But that is a very old story. When she was ill and you were so kind to her, she wanted to make you some return, and, not being herself at the time, scribbled 'Howards End' on a piece of paper. I went into it thoroughly, and, as it was clearly fanciful, I set it aside, little knowing what my Margaret would be to me in the future."

Margaret was silent. Something shook her life in its inmost recesses, and she shivered.

"I didn't do wrong, did I?" he asked, bending down.

"You didn't, darling. Nothing has been done wrong."

From the garden came laughter. "Here they are at last!" exclaimed Henry, disengaging himself with a smile. Helen rushed into the gloom, holding Tom by one hand and carrying her baby on the other. There were shouts of infectious joy.

"The field's cut!" Helen cried excitedly—"the big meadow! We've seen to the very end, and it'll be such a crop of hay as never!"

—E. M. FORSTER, *Howard's End*

"Yes, Jo, I think your harvest will be a good one," began Mrs. March, frightening away a big black cricket that was staring Teddy out of countenance.

"Not half so good as yours, mother. Here it is, and we never can thank you enough for the patient sowing and

Detail of the last page of the original manuscript of E. M. Forster's *Howard's End*. (King's College Library, Cambridge) reaping you have done," cried Jo, with the loving impetuosity which she never could outgrow.

"I hope there will be more wheat and fewer tares every year," said Amy softly.

"A large sheaf, but I know there's room in your heart for it, Marmee dear," added Meg's tender voice.

Touched to the heart, Mrs. March could only stretch out her arms as if to gather children and grandchildren to herself, and say, with face and voice full of motherly love, gratitude, and humility. "O my girls, however long you may live, I never can wish you a greater happiness than this!"

—LOUISA MAY ALCOTT, *Little Women*

My sisters and I stand, arms around each other, laughing and wiping the tears from each other's eyes. The flash of the Polaroid goes off and my father hands me the snapshot. My sisters and I watch quietly together, eager to see what develops.

The gray-green surface changes to the bright colors of our three images, sharpening and deepening all at once. And although we don't speak, I know we all see it: Together we look like our mother. Her same eyes, her same mouth, open in surprise to see, at last, her long-cherished wish.

—AMY TAN, *The Joy Luck Club*

(Extract from a letter from George Lawrence Esq., C.M.G., of His Majesty's Nigerian Civil Service, to Colonel Henri de Beaujolais, XIXth

African Army Corps. Michael "Beau" Geste has died, having confessed stealing a fake "Blue Water" stone that Lady Brandon, in fear of her late husband, had had made when she was forced to sell the real stone.)

"And the remaining piece of news is that I do most sincerely hope that you will be able to come over to England in June.

"You are the best man I know, Jolly, and I want you to be my Best Man, a desire heartily shared by Lady Brandon.

"Fancy, old cabbage, after more than thirty years of devotion! . . . I feel like a boy!

"And that fine boy, John, is going to marry the 'so beautiful child' whom you remembered. Lady Brandon is being a fairy godmother to them, indeed. I think she feels she is somehow doing something for Michael by smoothing their path so. . . ."

—PERCIVAL CHRISTOPHER WREN, *Beau Geste*

(After her infidelities on their trip to Europe, Samuel Dodsworth leaves Fran, his wife of twenty-three years, for the understanding, mature Edith Cortright.)

He came out of his silence with a consciousness that Edith was watching him. She said lightly, "You enjoy being sad about her! But hereafter, every time there is a music, I shall also think of Cecil Cortright. How handsome he was! He spoke five languages! How impatient I was with him! How I failed him! How virtuous it makes me feel to flay myself! What a splendid, uncommon grief I have! Dear Sam! . . . What a job it is to give up the superiority of being miserable and self-sacrificing!"

He stared, he pondered, he suddenly laughed, and in that laughter found a youthfulness he had never known in his solemn youth.

He was, indeed, so confidently happy that he completely forgot Fran and he did not again yearn over her, for almost two days.

—SINCLAIR LEWIS, *Dodsworth*

3 ❧ HOPE SPRINGS

argaret Mitchell is said to have written the last scene of *Gone with the Wind* first. It was a technique she had used in writing mystery stories, in which she worked backward from the solution to the crime, and although she was to rethink and eliminate many chapters of the book, this last scene remained intact. When her editor read the ending, in which Rhett has seemingly left his wife, Scarlett, forever, he felt it was too harsh. She agreed to soften it, but she refused to make it conventionally happy. After all, there was no doubt in Margaret Mitchell's mind that Scarlett would get Rhett back again. Her world may have come crashing down around her, but Scarlett had not given up, and the last words from her lips represent a final instance of her great courage, or as Margaret Mitchell herself called it, her "gumption." For Scarlett, whose strength came first from within, and then

from the land, there was always tomorrow, always Tara, and therefore, always hope.

Hope makes a good breakfast, Henry Fielding notes in *Tom Jones*. Hope also makes a good ending, whether it comes to the hero innocently wronged or to the hero redeemed from a life of wickedness. Either way, it means that a lesson has been learned, and the hero has moved from the point at which we first met him to the point where we must leave him. This movement is a vital element of the novel, as it is of the drama, story ballet, and opera.

Hope is the hero turning his back on the life he has always lived and venturing into the world, like Joel Knox in Truman Capote's *Other Voices, Other Rooms*: "She beckoned to him, shining and silver, and he knew he must go: unafraid, not hesitating, he paused only at the garden's edge where, as though he'd forgotten something, he stopped and looked back at the bloomless, descending blue, at the boy he had left behind." Or marching into the sunset as in *The Peaceable Kingdom*, by Jan de Hartog: "The red speck of the feathers on his Quaker hat was the last of him to vanish in the infinite prairie of light and love." Hope is a timid heroine daring to try something of which she was not before capable, as in Booth Tarkington's *Alice Adams*: "She looked up and down the street quickly, and then, with a little heave of the shoulders, she went bravely in, under the sign, and began to climb the wooden steps. Half-way up the shadows were heaviest, but after that the place began to seem brighter. There was an open window overhead somewhere, she found, and the steps at the top were gay with sunshine."

Hope can mean redemption, as for Konstantine Levin in *Anna Karenina*: ". . . my life now, my whole life apart from anything that can happen to me, every minute of it is no more meaningless, as it was before, but it has the positive meaning of goodness, which I have the power to put into it." Or an awareness of the vastness of the universe or the insistent cycle of Nature as an omen of good, as with Mr. Lockwood in *Wuthering Heights*: "I lingered round them, under that benign sky: watched the moths fluttering among the heath and hare-bells; listened to the soft wind breathing through the grass; and wondered how any one could ever imagine unquiet slumbers for the sleepers in that quiet earth."

Finally, hope can be symbolic, as in Conrad's *An Outcast of the Islands*, where a drunken Almayer assaults the Night and the fugitive Willems:

". . . Where are you, Willems? Hey? . . . Hey? . . . Where there is no mercy for you—I hope!"

"Hope," repeated in a whispering echo the startled forests, the river, and the hills; and Almayer, who stood waiting, with a smile of tipsy attention on his lips, heard no other answer.

Tomorrow and Tomorrow and Tomorrow ↩
The hero looks to a bright new day.

She felt vaguely comforted, strengthened by the picture, and some of her hurt and frantic regret was pushed from the top of her mind. She stood for a moment remembering small things, the avenue of dark cedars leading to Tara, the banks of cape jessamine bushes, vivid green against the white walls, the fluttering white curtains. And Mammy would be there. Suddenly she wanted Mammy desperately, as she had wanted her when she was a little girl, wanted the broad bosom on which to lay her head, the gnarled black hand on her hair. Mammy, the last link with the old days.

With the spirit of her people who would not know defeat, even when it stared them in the face, she raised her chin. She could get Rhett back. She knew she could. There had never been a man she couldn't get, once she set her mind upon him.

"I'll think of it all tomorrow, at Tara. I can stand it then. Tomorrow, I'll think of some way to get him back. After all, tomorrow is another day."

—MARGARET MITCHELL, *Gone with the Wind*

. . . What was it inside me that had turned pursuit and clutching into love, and then turned it inside out again? What was it that had turned winning into losing, and los-ing—who knows—into winning? I was sure I had loved Brenda, though standing there, I knew I couldn't any longer. And I knew it would be a long while before I made love to anyone the way I had made love to her. With anyone else, could I summon up such a passion? Whatever spawned my love for her, had that spawned such lust too? If she had only been slightly *not* Brenda . . . but then would I have loved her?

I looked hard at the image of me, at that darkening of the glass, and then my gaze pushed through it, over the cool floor, to a broken wall of books, imperfectly shelved.

I did not look very much longer, but took a train that got me into Newark just as the sun was rising on the first day of the Jewish New Year. I was back in plenty of time for work.

—PHILIP ROTH, *Goodbye, Columbus*

When I awoke it was early morning. I lay looking straight up at the blue-green sky with its translucent shawl of mist; like a tiny orb of crystal, solitary and serene, Venus shone through the haze above the quiet ocean. I heard children chattering nearby. I stirred. *"Izzy, he's awake!"* *"G'wan, yah mutha's mustache!"* *"Fuuu-ck you!"* Blessing my resurrection, I realized that the children had covered me with sand, protectively, and that I lay as safe as a mummy beneath this fine, enveloping overcoat. It was then that in my mind I inscribed the words: *'Neath cold sand I dreamed of death / but woke at dawn to see / in glory, the bright, the morning star.*

This was not judgment day—only morning. Morning: excellent and fair.

—WILLIAM STYRON, *Sophie's Choice*

. . . Naturally, at first it would only be a tedious, tiring job, it wouldn't prevent me from existing or from feeling that I exist. But a time would have to come when the book would be written, would be behind me, and I think that a little of its light would fall over my past. Then, through it, I might be ·able to recall my life without repugnance. Perhaps one day, thinking about this very moment, about this dismal moment at which I am waiting, round-shouldered, for it to be time to get on the train, perhaps I might feel my heart beat faster and say to myself: "It was on that day, at that moment that it all started." And I might succeed—in the past, simply in the past—in accepting myself.

Night is falling. On the first floor of the Hôtel Printania two windows have just lighted up. The yard of the New Station smells strongly of damp wood: tomorrow it will rain over Bouville.

—JEAN-PAUL SARTRE, *Nausea*

(Dr. Laurence Carroll returns to a small practice in Scotland, coming to terms with his pretensions to a great career and marrying a childhood friend pregnant with his child.)
"What the devil do you think you're doing, making all that bloody racket? I'm the new doctor here and I won't have it. Come in quietly or I'll throw your cards back at you." Dead silence.

They came in quietly.

"Now, who's first?" I said, sitting down at the desk.

An old gammer of about seventy struggled in—black mutch, tartan plaid, worn but genteel black gloves. As she settled herself, wheezing away, I looked at her in silence, waiting for what must come, knowing her for what she was, a seasoned veteran of the welfare medical service, bursting with arthritis, neuritis and bronchitis, with bunions and a probable varicose ulcer and, from the way she sat, constipation and piles. Could I stand it—the bitter medicine as before? Yes, with Dingwall sitting on my neck, Frank hanging round it, and that little package in the kitchen to be looked after, I would have to stick it out. At least, I would have to try.

—A. J. CRONIN, *A Pocketful of Rye*

(Professor Godfrey St. Peter is saved from suicide by an old German seamstress with whom he shares an office and is encouraged to continue to live.)

His temporary release from consciousness seemed to have been beneficial. He had let something go—and it was gone: something very precious, that he could not consciously have relinquished, probably. He doubted whether his family would ever realize that he was not the same man they had said good-bye to; they would be too happily preoccupied with their own affairs. If his apathy hurt them, they could not possibly be so much hurt as he had been already. At least, he felt the ground under his feet. He thought he knew where he was, and that he could face with fortitude the *Berengaria* and the future.

—WILLA CATHER, *The Professor's House*

When they were going over the first sand hill, Lov looked back through the rear curtain and saw the Lester place. The tall brick chimney standing blackened and tomb-like in the early morning sunlight was the only thing that he could see.

Dude took his hand off the horn-button and looked back at Lov.

"I reckon I'll get me a mule somewhere and some seed-cotton and guano, and grow me a crop of cotton this year," Dude said. "It feels to me like it's going to be a good year for cotton. Maybe I could grow me a bale to the acre, like Pa was always talking about doing."

—ERSKINE CALDWELL, *Tobacco Road*

It was certain that, in days soon to come, I should go home, those feelings flooding back, as alive as ever in the past, as I thought of cables or telephone calls. As alive as ever in the past. That was the price of the "I" which would not die.

But I had lived with that so long. I had lived with much else too, and now I could recognise it. This wasn't an end: though, if I had thought so, looking at the house, I should have needed to propitiate Fate, remembering so many others' luck, Francis Getliffe's and the rest, and the comparison with mine. I had lived with much else that I would have had, and begged to have, again. That night would be a happy one. This wasn't an end.

(Who would dare to look in the mirror of his future?)

There would be other nights when I should go to sleep, looking forward to tomorrow.

—C. P. SNOW, *Strangers and Brothers* [*Last Things*]

(King Arthur hopes for a day when he would return to Gramarye with a new Round Table.)

But it was too late for another effort then. For that time it was his destiny to die, or, as some say, to be carried off to Avilion, where he could wait for better days. For that time it was Lancelot's fate and Guenever's to take the tonsure and the veil, while Mordred must be slain. The fate of this man or that man was less than a drop, although it was a sparkling one, in the great blue motion of the sunlit sea.

The cannons of his adversary were thundering in the tattered morning when the Majesty of England drew himself up to meet the future with a peaceful heart.

EXPLICIT LIBER REGIS QUONDAM REGISQUE
FUTURI

THE BEGINNING

—T. H. WHITE, *The Once and Future King*

Hope Against Hope ⟿
The hero finds redemption.

(The gamekeeper writes a letter to his lover, Lady Constance Chatterley, while they are separated, waiting for the divorce that will unite them.)

"Never mind, never mind, we won't get worked up. We really trust in the little flame, in the unnamed god that shields it from being blown out. There's so much of you here with me, really, that it's a pity you aren't all here.

"Never mind about Sir Clifford. If you don't hear anything from him, never mind. He can't really do anything to you. Wait, he will want to get rid of you at last, to cast you out. And if he doesn't, we'll manage to keep clear of him. But he will. In the end he will want to spew you out as the abominable thing.

"Now I can't even leave off writing to you.

"But a great deal of us is together, and we can but abide by it, and steer our courses to meet soon. John Thomas says good night to lady Jane, a little droopingly, but with a hopeful heart."

—D. H. LAWRENCE, *Lady Chatterley's Lover*

I might go to Canada eventually, but I think I'll stop along the Columbia on the way. I'd like to check around Portland and Hood River and the Dalles to see if there's any of the guys I used to know back in the village who haven't drunk themselves goofy. I'd like to see what they've been doing since the government tried to buy their right to be Indians. I've even heard that some of the tribe have took to building their old ramshackle wood scaffolding all over that big million-dollar hydroelectric dam, and are spearing salmon in the spillway. I'd give something to see that. Mostly, I'd just like to look over the country around the gorge again, just to bring some of it clear in my mind again.

I been away a long time.

—KEN KESEY, *One Flew Over the Cuckoo's Nest*

(A young, divorced New York magazine writer, hooked on cocaine, begs for bread and begins to put his life back together.)

"Could I have some? A roll or something?"

"Get outa here."

"I'll trade you my sunglasses," you say. You take off your shades and hand them up to him. "Ray-Bans. I lost the case." He tries them on, shakes his head a few times and then takes them off. He folds the glasses and puts them in his shirt pocket.

"You're crazy," he says. Then he looks back into the ware-house. He picks up a bag of hard rolls and throws it at your feet.

You get down on your knees and tear open the bag. The smell of warm dough envelops you. The first bite sticks in your throat and you almost gag. You will have to go slowly. You will have to learn everything all over again.

—JAY MCINERNEY, *Bright Lights, Big City*

(The wily English barrister Sydney Carton is redeemed by taking the place of the Frenchman Charles Darnay on the scaffold because of his devotion to Darnay's wife, Lucie.)

". . . I see her, an old woman, weeping for me on the anniversary of this day. I see her and her husband, their course done, lying side by side in their last earthly bed, and I know that each was not more honoured and held sacred in the other's soul, than I was in the souls of both.

"I see that child who lay upon her bosom and who bore my name, a man winning his way up in that path of life which once was mine. I see him winning it so well, that my name is made illustrious there by the light of his. I see the blots I threw upon it, faded away. I see him, foremost of just judges and honoured men, bringing a boy of my name, with a forehead that I know and golden hair, to this place—then fair to look upon, with not a trace of this day's disfigurement—and I hear him tell the child my story, with a tender and a faltering voice.

"It is a far, far better thing that I do, than I have ever done; it is a far, far better rest that I go to, than I have ever known."

—CHARLES DICKENS, *A Tale of Two Cities*

(Abel has avenged the death of the jungle girl Rima, whom he loved, and returns with her ashes to the Venezuelan coast, from the forbidden forest.)

. . . In those darkest days in the forest I had her as a visitor—a Rima of the mind, whose words when she spoke reflected my despair. Yet even then I was not entirely without hope. Heaven itself, she said, could not undo that which I had done; and she also said that if I forgave myself Heaven would say no word, nor would she. That is my philosophy still; prayers, austerities, good works—they avail nothing, and there is no intercession, and outside of the soul there is no forgiveness in heaven or earth for sin. Nevertheless there is a way, which every soul can find out for itself—even the most rebellious, the most darkened with crime and tormented by remorse. In that way I have walked; and, self-forgiven and self-absolved, I know that here where her ashes are—I know that her divine eyes would no longer refuse to look into mine, since the sorrow which seemed eternal and would have slain me to see would not now be in them.

—W. H. Hudson, *Green Mansions*

(Jack Flowers, an expatriate in Singapore, a water clerk and a pimp, considers his future.)

. . . So my life was only half gone. I would celebrate the coming glory with an expensive drink at Raffles, down the road, and, time permitting, do a spot of work before I put in an appearance at the Bandung. Children with bright lanterns moved along the promenade toward me, swinging their blobs of light. I blessed them simply, wishing them well with a nod.

There was another admirer. A woman in a white dress, with a camera slung over her shoulder, leaned against the sea rail twenty feet away. When the children passed by, she approached me, smiling.

"What beautiful children," she said. "Are they Chinese?"

"Yeah," I said. "But they should be in bed at this hour."

"So should I," said the woman, and she laughed gently. She was a corker. She looked across the street and held her fingers to her mouth and kissed them in concentration. "Oh, hell," she said, "I'm lost."

"No, you're not," I said.

"Hey, you're an American, too," she said. "Do you have a minute?"

"Lady, believe me," I said, and a high funny note of joy,

recovered hope, warbled in my ears as I pronounced the
adventurous sentence, "I've got all the time in the world."
—PAUL THEROUX, *Saint Jack*

*(His life threatened if he gives any more pacifist speeches, Anthony
Beavis overcomes his cowardice and goes to speak at a meeting in
Battersea.)*
The clock struck seven. Slowly and cautiously he allowed
himself to lapse out of the light, back through the darkness
into the broken gleams and shadows of everyday existence.
He rose at last and went to the kitchen to prepare himself
some food. There was not much time; the meeting was at
eight, and it would take him a good half-hour to reach the
hall. He put a couple of eggs to boil, and sat down meanwhile to bread and cheese. Dispassionately, and with a serene
lucidity, he thought of what was in store for him. Whatever
it might be, he knew now that all would be well.
—ALDOUS HUXLEY, *Eyeless in Gaza*

*(Running from the police after killing a man who was raiding the
camp of homeless men where he lived, Francis Phelan takes refuge
with his wife Annie.)*
If they were on to him, well that's all she wrote. Katie bar the
door. Too wet to plow. He'd head where it was warm, where
he would never again have to run from men or weather.

The empyrean, which is not spatial at all, does not move
and has no poles. It girds, with light and love, the primum

mobile, the utmost and swiftest of the material heavens.
Angels are manifested in the primum mobile.

But if they weren't on to him, then he'd mention it to
Annie someday (she already had the thought, he could tell
that) about setting up the cot down in Danny's room, when
things got to be absolutely right, and straight.

That room of Danny's had some space to it.

And it got the morning light too.

It was a mighty nice little room.

—WILLIAM KENNEDY, *Ironweed*

In time he lay down on his bed looking at the ceiling curiously, a splotch of brown—a leak in the roof, no doubt. As
he began to observe the marks on the ceiling, gradually the
inner agitation, the troubled surface of his mind, grew quiet.
One by one the voices were silenced. He thought of that last
conversation. The thing he could do for her, the whole
meaning of their relationship, he saw would lie in his work.
And there is so much to do, he thought. There is so much to
do that I must begin at once. Where there is action possible
there can be no despair.

The loneliness would come later. It is harder to get
beyond it. But in the end he would come to see that one
does not find this kind of love, built on understanding, and
ever lose it. It would not matter now where he was, she
would always be there. It was a way of living he had found.
It was the means of living, not with her, but with himself.

—MAY SARTON, *The Single Hound*

(Tom, now at Oxford, hears the Master of Rugby has died and visits the chapel where he is buried.)

And let us not be hard on him, if at that moment his soul is fuller of the tomb and him who lies there, than of the altar and Him of whom it speaks. Such stages have to be gone through, I believe, by all young and brave souls, who must win their way through hero-worship, to the worship of Him who is the King and Lord of heroes. For it is only through our mysterious human relationships, through the love and tenderness and purity of mothers, and sisters, and wives, through the strength and courage and wisdom of fathers, and brothers, and teachers, that we can come to the knowledge of Him, in whom alone the love, and the tenderness, and the purity, and the strength, and the courage, and the wisdom of all these dwell for ever and ever in perfect fulness.

—AN OLD BOY [Thomas Hughes],
Tom Brown's School-Days

(Amory Blaine, now poor, listening to the sound of bells amid the towers of Princeton, thinks of the next generation, about to begin the struggles of their lives.)

Amory, sorry for them, was still not sorry for himself—art, politics, religion, whatever his medium should be, he knew he was safe now, free from all hysteria—he could accept what was acceptable, roam, grow, rebel, sleep deep through many nights. . . .

There was no God in his heart, he knew; his ideas were still in riot; there was ever the pain of memory; the regret for his lost youth—yet the waters of disillusion had left a deposit on his soul, responsibility and a love of life, the faint stirring of old ambitions and unrealized dreams. But—oh, Rosalind! Rosalind! . . .

"It's all a poor substitute at best," he said sadly.

And he could not tell why the struggle was worth while, why he had determined to use to the utmost himself and his heritage from the personalities he had passed. . . .

He stretched out his arms to the crystalline, radiant sky.

"I know myself," he cried, "but that is all."

—F. SCOTT FITZGERALD, *This Side of Paradise*

The ticket collector looked at me.

"You gettin' on this train?" I shook my head, taking a step forward at the same time.

I did not wait for the train to leave. I transferred the suitcase to my left hand and walked out of the station. In Bull Ring I stopped and lit a cigarette and buttoned up my coat. The suitcase felt absurdly light. I began to breathe great gusts of air, but there was little air to breathe.

I walked across Bull Ring and up Moorgate. Suddenly I began to feel excited and buoyant, and I was almost running by the time I reached Town Square. I began to whistle "March of the Movies" and to march in step with it. There was nobody about. When I came to the War Memorial I transferred my suitcase to my right hand and at the correct moment I saluted with the left—up, two, three, down, two, three, head erect, shoulders back. I brought the whistling to a huffing crescendo and wheeled smartly into Infirmary Street. I dropped into a normal step, and then I began the slow walk home.

—KEITH WATERHOUSE, *Billy Liar*

(Farragut, who has just escaped from Falconer Prison by taking the place of a corpse in a body bag, is given a raincoat by a stranger.) Farragut put his arms into the sleeves and settled the coat around his shoulders. "Perfect, perfect," exclaimed the stranger. "It's a perfect fit. You know, you look like a million dollars in that coat. You look like you just deposited a million dollars in the bank and was walking out of the bank, very slowly, you know, like you was going to meet some broad in a very expensive restaurant and buy her lunch. It's a perfect fit."

"Thank you very much," said Farragut. He stood and shook the stranger's hand. "I'm getting off at the next stop."

"Well, that's all right," said the stranger. "You got my telephone number. I'm in from ten to four, maybe a little later. I don't go out for lunch, but don't call me at my sister's."

Farragut walked to the front of the bus and got off at the next stop. Stepping from the bus onto the street, he saw that he had lost his fear of falling and all other fears of that nature. He held his head high, his back straight, and walked along nicely. Rejoice, he thought, rejoice.

—JOHN CHEEVER, *Falconer*

(Searching for the wartime grave of her brother Julio with her parents and husband, René, Chichí Lacour embraces a hopeful future.)

. . . René was standing at the foot of the knoll, and several times after a sweeping glance at the numberless mounds around them, she looked thoughtfully at him, as though trying to establish a relationship between her husband and those below. And he had exposed his life in combats just as these men had done! . . .

"And you, my poor darling," she continued aloud. "At this very moment you, too, might be lying here under a heap of earth with a wooden cross at your head, just like these poor unfortunates!"

The sub-lieutenant smiled sadly. Yes, it was so.

"Come here; climb up here!" said Chichí impetuously. "I want to give you something!"

As soon as he approached her, she flung her arms around his neck, pressed him against the warm softness of her breast, exhaling a perfume of life and love, and kissed him passionately without a thought of her brother, without seeing her aged parents grieving below them and longing to die. . . . And her skirts, freed by the breeze, molded her figure in the superb sweep of the curves of a Grecian vase.

—Vicente Blasco Ibañez, *The Four Horsemen of the Apocalypse,* trans. Charlotte Brewster Jordan

So it came to pass that as he trudged from the place of blood and wrath his soul changed. He came from hot plowshares to prospects of clover tranquilly, and it was as if hot plowshares were not. Scars faded as flowers.

It rained. The procession of weary soldiers became a bedraggled train, despondent and muttering, marching with churning effort in a trough of liquid brown mud under a low, wretched sky. Yet the youth smiled, for he saw that the world was a world for him, though many discovered it to be made of oaths and walking sticks. He had rid himself of the red sickness of battle. The sultry nightmare was in the past. He had been an animal blistered and sweating in the heat and pain of war. He turned now with a lover's thirst to images of tranquil skies, fresh meadows, cool brooks—an existence of soft and eternal peace.

Over the river a golden ray of sun came through the hosts of leaden rain clouds.

—STEPHEN CRANE, *The Red Badge of Courage*

Almayer shrugged his shoulders and walked back to the balustrade. He drank his own trade gin very seldom, but, when he did, a ridiculously small quantity of the stuff could induce him to assume a rebellious attitude towards the scheme of the universe. And now, throwing his body over the rail, he shouted impudently into the night, turning his face towards that far-off and invisible slab of imported granite upon which Lingard had thought fit to record God's mercy and Willems' escape.

"Father was wrong—wrong!" he yelled. "I want you to

smart for it. You must smart for it! Where are you, Willems? Hey? . . . Hey? . . . Where there is no mercy for you—I hope!"

"Hope," repeated in a whispering echo the startled forests, the river, and the hills; and Almayer, who stood waiting, with a smile of tipsy attention on his lips, heard no other answer.

—JOSEPH CONRAD, *An Outcast of the Islands*

(Having reunited the lovers Valentine and Maximilian Morrel, and left them his treasure, the Count, Edmond Dantès, sets sail with his beautiful Greek slave, Haydée.)

The eyes of both were fixed upon the spot indicated by the sailor, and on the blue line separating the sky from the Mediterranean Sea they perceived a large white sail.

"Gone!" said Morrel: "Gone!—Adieu, my friend!—adieu, my father!"

"Gone!" murmured Valentine: "Adieu, my friend!—adieu, my sister!"

"Who can say whether we shall ever see them again?" said Morrel with tearful eyes.

"Maximilian," replied Valentine, "has not the count just told us that all human wisdom was contained in these two words,—*'Wait and hope.'*"

—ALEXANDRE DUMAS, *The Count of Monte Cristo*

(The greatness and name of the Buddenbrooks die out with the death of the young Hanno.)

"Hanno, little Hanno," went on Frau Permaneder, the tears flowing down over her soft faded cheeks. "Tom, Father, Grandfather, and all the rest! Where are they? We shall see them no more. Oh, it is so sad, so hard!"

"There will be a reunion," said Friederike Buddenbrook. She folded her hands in her lap, cast down her eyes, and put her nose in the air.

"Yes—they say so.—Oh, there are times, Friederike, when that is no consolation, God forgive me! When one begins to doubt—doubt justice and goodness—and everything. Life crushes so much in us, it destroys so many of our beliefs—! A reunion—if that were so—"

But now Sesemi Weichbrodt stood up, as tall as ever she could. She stood on tip-toe, rapped on the table; the cap shook on her old head.

"It *is so!*" she said, with her whole strength; and looked at them all with a challenge in her eyes.

She stood there, a victor in the good fight which all her life she had waged against the assaults of Reason: hump-backed, tiny, quivering with the strength of her convictions, a little prophetess, admonishing and inspired.

—THOMAS MANN, *Buddenbrooks,*
trans. H. T. Lowe-Porter

(Charlie Citrine, now a Pulitzer Prize–winning writer, arranges to have his late mentor, Von Humboldt Fleisher, reburied next to his mother.)

Menasha and I went toward the limousine. The side of his foot brushed away some of last autumn's leaves and he said, looking through his goggles, "What's this, Charlie, a spring flower?"

"It is. I guess it's going to happen after all. On a warm day like this everything looks ten times deader."

"So it's a little flower," Menasha said. "They used to tell one about a kid asking his grumpy old man when they were walking in the park, 'What's the name of this flower, Papa?' and the old guy is peevish and he yells, 'How should I know? Am I in the millinery business?' Here's another, but what do you suppose they're called, Charlie?"

"Search me," I said. "I'm a city boy myself. They must be crocuses."

—SAUL BELLOW, *Humboldt's Gift*

. . . There's bound to be trouble in store for me every day of my life, because trouble it's always been and always will be. Born drunk and married blind, misbegotten into a strange and crazy world, dragged-up through the dole and into the war with a gas-mask on your clock, and the sirens rattling into you every night while you rot with scabies in an air-raid shelter. Slung into khaki at eighteen, and when they let you out, you sweat again in a factory, grabbing for an extra pint, doing women at the weekend and getting to know whose husbands are on the night-shift, working with rotten guts and an aching spine, and nothing for it but money to drag you back there every Monday morning.

Well, it's a good life and a good world, all said and done, if you don't weaken, and if you know that the big wide world hasn't heard from you yet, no, not by a long way, though it won't be long now.

The float bobbed more violently than before and, with a grin on his face, he began to wind in the reel.

—ALAN SILLITOE, *Saturday Night and Sunday Morning*

"Why, my love, you talk as though you were fifty. You've got all your life before you. You mustn't be down-hearted."

Kitty shook her head and slowly smiled.

"I'm not. I have hope and courage. The past is finished; let the dead bury their dead. It's all uncertain, life and whatever is to come to me, but I enter upon it with a light and buoyant heart. There's so much I want to know; I want to read and I want to learn. I see in front of me the glorious fun of the world, people and music and dancing, and I see its beauty, the sea and the palm-trees, the sunrise and the sunset and the starry night. It's all confused, but vaguely I discern a pattern, and I see before me an inexhaustible richness, the mystery and the strangeness of everything, compassion and charity, the Way and the Wayfarer, and perhaps in the end— God."

—W. SOMERSET MAUGHAM, *The Painted Veil*

. . . First of course I'm going to have my baby. There is a sort of ashram further up, and I'm told they might take me in. I have seen some of the swamis from the ashram when they come down to the bazaar to do their shopping. They are very much respected in the town because of the good lives they lead. They are completely dedicated to studying the philosophy of those ancient writings that had their birth up in the highest heights of these mountains I cannot yet see. The swamis are cheerful men and they laugh and joke in booming voices with the people in the bazaar. I'm told that any sincere seeker can go up to the ashram, and they will allow one to stay for as long as one wants. Only most people come down again quite soon because of the cold and the austere living conditions.

Next time I meet a swami I shall speak to him and ask for permission to come up. I don't know yet how long I shall stay. In any case, it will have to be some time because of my condition which will make it more and more difficult to get down again, even if I should want to.

—RUTH PRAWER JHABVALA, *Heat and Dust*

(Alone again, Mildred Lathbury weighs her future: minding the Vicar, Julian Malory, and proofreading for Everard Bone.)
And then another picture came into my mind. Julian Malory, standing by the electric fire, wearing his speckled mackintosh, holding a couple of ping-pong bats and quoting a not very appropriate bit of Keats. He might need to be protected from the women who were going to live in his house. So,

what with my duty there and the work I was going to do for Everard, it seemed as if I might be going to have what Helena called "a full life" after all.

—BARBARA PYM, *Excellent Women*

"This new feeling has not changed me, has not made me happy and enlightened all of a sudden, as I had dreamed, just like the feeling for my child. There was no surprise in this either. Faith—or not faith—I don't know what it is—but this feeling has come just as imperceptibly through suffering, and has taken firm root in my soul.

"I shall go on in the same way, losing my temper with Ivan the coachman, falling into angry discussions, expressing my opinions tactlessly; there will be still the same wall between the holy of holies of my soul and other people, even my wife; I shall still go on scolding her for my own terror, and being remorseful for it; I shall still be as unable to understand with my reason why I pray, and I shall still go on praying; but my life now, my whole life apart from anything that can happen to me, every minute of it is no more meaningless, as it was before, but it has the positive meaning of goodness, which I have the power to put into it."

—COUNT LEO TOLSTOY, *Anna Karenina,*
trans. Constance Garnett

That being so, of this I am certain; that it will be impossible to free myself, to escape from this world, unless in peace and amity I can take every shred of it, every friend and every enemy, all that these eyes have seen, these senses discovered with me. I *know* that. And perhaps for that very reason, in spite of the loving gratitude that overcomes me at the thought of what my existence might have been, I sometimes dread the ease and quiet and seclusion in which I live. And this tale itself? As Mrs. Monnerie had said, what is it but once more to have drifted into being on show again—in a book? That is so; and so I must leave it, hoping against hope that one friend at any rate will consent in his love and wisdom to take me seriously, and to remember me, not with scorn or even with pity, but as if, life for life, we had shared the world on equal terms.

—WALTER DE LA MARE, *Memoirs of a Midget*

Into the Sunset ⌒

In search of happiness, the hero leaves for parts unknown.

And day came, and the song of waking birds, and the Square, bathed in the young pearl light of morning. And a wind stirred lightly in the Square, and, as he looked, Ben, like a fume of smoke, was melted into dawn.

And the angels on Gant's porch were frozen in hard marble silence, and at a distance life awoke, and there was a rattle of lean wheels, a slow clangor of shod hoofs. And he heard the whistle wail along the river.

Yet, as he stood for the last time by the angels of his father's porch, it seemed as if the Square already were far and lost; or, I should say, he was like a man who stands upon a hill above the town he has left, yet does not say "The town is near," but turns his eyes upon the distant soaring ranges.

—THOMAS WOLFE, *Look Homeward, Angel*

The young man's mind was carried away by his growing passion for dreams. One looking at him would not have thought him particularly sharp. With the recollection of little things occupying his mind he closed his eyes and leaned back in the car seat. He stayed that way for a long time and when he aroused himself and again looked out of the car window the town of Winesburg had disappeared and his life there had become but a background on which to paint the dreams of his manhood.

—SHERWOOD ANDERSON, *Winesburg, Ohio*

His mind was absolutely clear. He was like a camera waiting for its subject to enter focus. The wall yellowed in the meticulous setting of the October sun, and the windows were rippling mirrors of cold, seasonal color. Beyond one, someone was watching him. All of him was dumb except his eyes. They knew. And it was Randolph's window. Gradually the blinding sunset drained from the glass, darkened, and it was as if snow were falling there, flakes shaping snow-eyes, hair: a face trembled like a white beautiful moth, smiled. She beckoned to him, shining and silver, and he knew he must go: unafraid, not hesitating, he paused only at the garden's edge

The last two pages of the original notebook manuscript of Thomas Wolfe's *Look Homeward, Angel.* (Houghton Library, Harvard University, bMs Am 1883 [194–210]) where, as though he'd forgotten something, he stopped and looked back at the bloomless, descending blue, at the boy he had left behind.

—TRUMAN CAPOTE, *Other Voices, Other Rooms*

(Esther Greenwood is awaiting a final interview that will mean her dismissal from the asylum in which she has been treated.)
I had hoped, at my departure, I would feel sure and knowledgeable about everything that lay ahead—after all, I had been "analyzed." Instead, all I could see were question marks.

I kept shooting impatient glances at the closed boardroom door. My stocking seams were straight, my black shoes cracked, but polished, and my red wool suit flamboyant as my plans. Something old, something new. . . .

But I wasn't getting married. There ought, I thought, to be a ritual for being born twice—patched, retreaded and approved for the road, I was trying to think of an appropriate one when Doctor Nolan appeared from nowhere and touched me on the shoulder.

"All right, Esther."

I rose and followed her to the open door.

Pausing, for a brief breath, on the threshold, I saw the silver-haired doctor who had told me about the rivers and the Pilgrims on my first day, and the pocked, cadaverous face of Miss Huey, and eyes I thought I had recognized over white masks.

The eyes and the faces all turned themselves toward me,

and guiding myself by them, as by a magical thread, I stepped into the room.

—SYLVIA PLATH, *The Bell Jar*

"What do you think about it, Captain?" I asked at last. "I can really do anything that turns up. What am I saying? I would be a poor sort of chap if I couldn't do a little more than just what I was put to. I can take two watches at a stretch, if it comes to that. It would only do me good, and I could hold out all the same."

"All right, have a try at it. If it doesn't work, well, we can part in England."

"Of course," I reply in my delight, and I repeated over again that we could part in England if it didn't work.

And he set me to work. . . .

Out in the fjord I dragged myself up once, wet with fever and exhaustion, and gazed landwards, and bade farewell for the present to the town—to Christiania, where the windows gleamed so brightly in all the homes.

—KNUT HAMSUN, *Hunger,*
trans. George Egerton

So I had my last lunch at home, with my mother and Uncle Bhakcu and his wife. Then back along the hot road to Piarco where the plane was waiting. I recognized one of the customs' officers, and he didn't check my baggage.

The announcement came, a cold, casual thing.

I embraced my mother.

I said to Bhakcu, "Uncle Bhak, I didn't want to tell you before, but I think I hear your tappet knocking."

His eyes shone.

I left them all and walked briskly towards the aeroplane, not looking back, looking only at my shadow before me, a dancing dwarf on the tarmac.

—V. S. NAIPAUL, *Miguel Street*

I woke in the morning and prayed. My parents were not home. I made myself breakfast. I wandered about the apartment and walked the streets. I had lunch alone in the apartment and supper with my parents. I packed my bags. We stood at the door. My mother was crying. My father stood next to her, tall, heavy-shouldered, his eyes dark—and moist, I thought. He said nothing, but he shook my hand. "Please write," my mother said. "You'll write?" She looked tiny and fragile. "Have a safe journey, my Asher," she kept saying. "Have a safe journey."

I came out of the apartment house. It was cold and dark. I looked up. My parents stood framed in the living-room window. I hailed a cab and climbed inside. It pulled slowly away from the curb. I turned in the seat and looked out the rear window of the cab. My parents were still watching me through our living-room window.

—CHAIM POTOK, *My Name Is Asher Lev*

Sunrise finds him walking along a cement road between dumping grounds full of smoking rubbishpiles. The sun shines redly through the mist on rusty donkeyengines, skeleton trucks, wishbones of Fords, shapeless masses of corroding metal. Jimmy walks fast to get out of the smell. He is hungry; his shoes are beginning to raise blisters on his big toes. At a cross-road where the warning light still winks and winks, is a gasoline station, opposite it the Lightning Bug lunchwagon. Carefully he spends his last quarter on breakfast. That leaves him three cents for good luck, or bad for that matter. A huge furniture truck, shiny and yellow, has drawn up outside.

"Say will you give me a lift?" he asks the redhaired man at the wheel.

"How fur ye goin?"

"I dunno. . . . Pretty far."

—JOHN DOS PASSOS, *Manhattan Transfer*

(After trying unsuccessfully to marry and elevate herself socially, Alice crosses the threshold of Frincke's Business College, which before had seemed to her the end of hope and youth.)
Well, she was here at last! She looked up and down the street quickly, and then, with a little heave of the shoulders, she went bravely in, under the sign, and began to climb the wooden steps. Half-way up the shadows were heaviest, but after that the place began to seem brighter. There was an open window overhead somewhere, she found, and the steps at the top were gay with sunshine.

—BOOTH TARKINGTON, *Alice Adams*

Some time after midnight there is a thunderstorm and the last I see of the village is in the light of these explosions, knowing how harshly time will bear down on this ingenuous place. Lightning plays around the steeple of Christ Church, that symbol of our engulfing struggle with good and evil, and I repeat those words that were found in Leander's wallet after he drowned: "Let us consider that the soul of man is immortal, able to endure every sort of good and every sort of evil." A cavernous structure of sound, a sort of abyss in the stillness of the provincial night, opens along the whole length of heaven and the wooden roof under which I stand amplifies the noise of rain. I will never come back, and if I do there will be nothing left, there will be nothing left but the headstones to record what has happened; there will really be nothing at all.

—JOHN CHEEVER, *The Wapshot Scandal*

He pulled his cap lower down, made sure that his coat-collar covered his throat and neck, and walked with stirred imagination off into the driving rain.

"Cheerio, Frank," I called out as he turned the corner. I wondered what would be left of him by the time they had finished. Would they succeed in tapping and draining dry the immense subterranean reservoir of his dark inspired mind?

I watched him. He ignored the traffic-lights, walked diagonally across the wide wet road, then ran after a bus and leapt safely on to its empty platform.

And I with my books have not seen him since. It was like saying goodbye to a big part of me, for ever.

—ALAN SILLITOE,
The Loneliness of the Long-distance Runner

And at last I step out into the morning and I lock the door behind me. I cross the road and drop the keys into the old lady's mailbox. And I look up the road, where a few people stand, men and women, waiting for the morning bus. They are very vivid beneath the awakening sky, and the horizon beyond them is beginning to flame. The morning weighs on my shoulders with the dreadful weight of hope and I take the blue envelope which Jacques has sent me and tear it slowly into many pieces, watching them dance in the wind, watching the wind carry them away. Yet, as I turn and begin walking toward the waiting people, the wind blows some of them back on me.

—JAMES BALDWIN, *Giovanni's Room*

He could not kiss Juli because she was wearing a bourka, but he put his arms about her and held her close for a brief moment, before turning aside to change quickly into the clothes that Gul Baz had ready for him. It would not do to travel as a scribe, and when he mounted one of the ponies a few minutes later he was to all outward appearances an Afridi, complete with rifle, bandolier and tulwar, and the wicked razor-edged knife that is carried by all men of Afghanistan.

"I am ready," said Ash, "let us go. We have a long way to travel before dawn, and I can smell the morning."

They rode out together from the shadows of the trees, leaving the Bala Hissar and the glowing torch of the burning Residency behind them, and spurred away across the flat lands towards the mountains . . .

And it may even be that they found their Kingdom.

—M. M. KAYE, *The Far Pavilions*

(Buffalo McHair returns home to find a Quaker village of whites, blacks, and Indians all living together like the animals in the Peaceable Kingdom, and leaves a worship service to ride out into the prairie.)
It was high noon when he reached the crest of the hill where the prairie began. "Ah!" he said as he saw it. For a moment he stood still, dazzled by its vastness; then he flicked the reins and cantered down the slope into the man-high sawgrass, flushing a cloud of birds as Fury plunged into the waves.

The sky was clear and bright, the wind swept spinning whorls across the shimmering plain.

The red speck of the feathers on his Quaker hat was the last of him to vanish in the infinite prairie of light and love.

—JAN DE HARTOG, *The Peaceable Kingdom*

Garden felt very unhappy. Everything was so empty now that every one had gone; the spirit of desolation was abroad. Life was a thing of littering paper, of gaping forms, of dusty floors. He went down to the cliffs, and here the splendour of the day cheered him. It was amazingly warm for December. The sea in the cove sparkled and glittered, and even the black rock seemed to smile.

He stood above the cove and looked out to sea. . . .

Perrin, although he was a bit of an ass, was really a good sort. . . . He would behave more decently next term. He would make up a bit. . . . He was a queer beggar, Perrin, but he meant to be decent to him . . . next term.

His tiny figure made a black dot against the shining surface of the long, white road.

—HUGH WALPOLE, *Mr. Perrin and Mr. Traill*

By midnight he had left the road and the burning woods behind him and had come out on the highway once more. The moon, riding low above the field beside him, appeared and disappeared, diamond-bright, between patches of darkness. Intermittently the boy's jagged shadow slanted across the road ahead of him as if it cleared a rough path toward his goal. His singed eyes, black in their deep sockets, seemed already to envision the fate that awaited him but he moved steadily on, his face set toward the dark city, where the children of God lay sleeping.

—FLANNERY O'CONNOR, *The Violent Bear It Away*

He went out to watch the launching of the dawn strike. As streaks of light appeared in the east, pilots came on deck. Bundled like animals awakened from hibernation, they waddled purposefully to their jets. The last to climb aboard was Cag, stocky and round like a snowball. He checked each jet, then studied his own. Finally, as if there were nothing more he could do, he scrambled into his plane and waited. Majestically, the task force turned into the wind, the bull horn jangled and a voice in the gloom cried, "Launch jets."

Admiral Tarrant watched them go, two by two from the lashing catapult, planes of immortal beauty whipping into the air with flame and fury upon them. They did not waste fuel orbiting but screamed to the west, seeking new bridges in Korea.

—JAMES A. MICHENER, *The Bridges at Toko-ri*

He sat for a long time on the bench in the thickening dusk, his eyes never turning from the balcony. At length a light shone through the windows, and a moment later a man-servant came out on the balcony, drew up the awnings, and closed the shutters.

At that, as if it had been the signal he waited for, Newland Archer got up slowly and walked back alone to his hotel.

—EDITH WHARTON, *The Age of Innocence*

Heaven Knows ↜
Solace comes from the benign universe.

My walk home was lengthened by a diversion in the direction of the kirk. When beneath its walls, I perceived decay

The last two pages of an early outline of Edith Wharton's *The Age of Innocence*, in which Newland Archer marries, then separates from, Countess Olenska, and "May Welland marries some one else & nothing ever happens to him again." *(Yale Collection of American Literature, Beinecke Rare Book and Manuscript Library, Yale University)* had made progress, even in seven months: many a window showed black gaps deprived of glass; and slates jutted off, here and there, beyond the right line of the roof, to be gradually worked off in coming autumn storms.

I sought, and soon discovered, the three headstones on the slope next the moor: the middle one grey, and half buried in heath; Edgar Linton's only harmonized by the turf, and moss creeping up its foot; Heathcliff's still bare.

I lingered round them, under that benign sky: watched the moths fluttering among the heath and hare-bells; listened to the soft wind breathing through the grass; and wondered how any one could ever imagine unquiet slumbers for the sleepers in that quiet earth.

—EMILY BRONTË, *Wuthering Heights*

(Yevgeny Bazarov has died after contracting typhus from a scalpel used on one of his patients, his doctor father having been unable to save him.)

. . . Often from the little village not far off, two quite feeble old people come to visit it—a husband and wife. Supporting one another, they move to it with heavy steps; they go up to the railing, fall down, and remain on their knees, and long and bitterly they weep, and yearn, and intently they gaze at the dumb stone, under which their son is lying; they exchange some brief word, wipe away the dust from the stone, set straight a branch of a fir-tree, and pray again, and cannot tear themselves from this place, where they seem to be nearer to their son, to their memories of him. . . . Can it be that their prayers, their tears are fruitless? Can it be that love, sacred, devoted love, is not all-powerful? Oh, no! However passionate, sinning, and rebellious the heart hidden in the tomb, the flowers growing over it peep serenely at us with their innocent eyes; they tell us not of eternal peace alone, of that great peace of "indifferent" nature; they tell us, too, of eternal reconciliation and of life without end.

—IVAN TURGENEV, *Fathers and Sons,*
trans. Constance Garnett

With death so near, Mother must have felt like someone on the brink of freedom, ready to start life all over again. No one, no one in the world had any right to weep for her. And I, too, felt ready to start life all over again. It was as if that great rush of anger had washed me clean, emptied me of hope, and, gazing up at the dark sky spangled with its signs and stars, for the first time, the first, I laid my heart open to the benign indifference of the universe. To feel it so like myself, indeed, so brotherly, made me realize that I'd been happy, and that I was happy still. For all to be accomplished, for me to feel less lonely, all that remained to hope was that on the day of my execution there should be a huge crowd of spectators and that they should greet me with howls of execration.

—ALBERT CAMUS, *The Stranger,* trans. Stuart Gilbert

Laura lifted on her knees and took her Aunt Ellen around the neck. She held her till they swayed together. Would Aunt Ellen remember it against her, that she had run away from her when she fainted? Of course Aunt Ellen would never find out about the rosy pin. Should she tell her, and suffer? Yes. No. She touched Aunt Ellen's cheek with three anxious, repaying kisses.

"Oh, beautiful!" Another star fell in the sky.

Laura let go and ran forward a step. "I saw that one too."

"Did you?" said somebody—Uncle George.

"I saw where it fell," said Laura, bragging and in reassurance.

She turned again to them, both arms held out to the radiant night.

—EUDORA WELTY, *Delta Wedding*

Hilary followed the Judge down the passageway and up the stairs to the main deck. It was a cool evening, and across the Hudson an enormous, red sun was setting over the black hulk of New Jersey and turning the dirty water to a golden gray. The city behind him seemed gaunt and grim and somehow spent, yet at the same time sullen, defiant, as if the warehouses and towers, like the huge billboards along the river drive, were proclaiming, under that darkening sky, that they existed, quite as importantly—however little that was—as all the more ancient and beautiful places to which the murky waters around them might ultimately flow. He left the Judge, who was looking for John, and walked to the stern of

the ship to take in, over the water, the full glory of the twilight. His heart was very full, but a part of that weight was
hope. They were going away, all of them, and leaving Sophie
to him.

—LOUIS AUCHINCLOSS, *A World of Profit*

. . . So quietly flows the Seine that one hardly notices its
presence. It is always there, quiet and unobtrusive, like a
great artery running through the human body. In the wonderful peace that fell over me it seemed as if I had climbed to
the top of a high mountain; for a little while I would be able
to look around me, to take in the meaning of the landscape.

Human beings make a strange fauna and flora. From a distance they appear negligible; close up they are apt to appear
ugly and malicious. More than anything they need to be surrounded with sufficient space—space even more than time.

The sun is setting. I feel this river flowing through me—its
past, its ancient soil, the changing climate. The hills gently
girdle it about: its course is fixed.

—HENRY MILLER, *Tropic of Cancer*

Soon it will be evening and the clear night sky will be dusted
thickly with summer stars. I shall be here, as always, smoking
by the water. I have decided to leave Clea's last letter unan-
swered. I no longer wish to coerce anyone, to make

promises, to think of life in terms of compacts, resolutions, covenants. It will be up to Clea to interpret my silence according to her own needs and desires, to come to me if she has need or not, as the case may be. Does not everything depend on our interpretation of the silence around us?

—LAWRENCE DURRELL, *Justine*

Dawn was breaking over everything in colours at once clear and timid; as if Nature made a first attempt at yellow and a first attempt at rose. A breeze blew so clean and sweet, that one could not think that it blew from the sky; it blew rather through some hole in the sky. Syme felt a simple surprise when he saw rising all round him on both sides of the road the red, irregular buildings of Saffron Park. He had no idea that he had walked so near London. He walked by instinct along one white road, on which early birds hopped and sang, and found himself outside a fenced garden. There he saw the sister of Gregory, the girl with the gold-red hair, cutting lilac before breakfast, with the great unconscious gravity of a girl.

—G. K. CHESTERTON, *The Man Who Was Thursday*

Yes, it is the dawn that has come. The titihoya wakes from sleep, and goes about its work of forlorn crying. The sun tips with light the mountains of Ingeli and East Griqualand. The great valley of the Umzimkulu is still in darkness, but the light will come there. Ndotsheni is still in darkness, but the light will come there also. For it is the dawn that has come, as it has come for a thousand centuries, never failing. But when that dawn will come, of our emancipation, from the fear of bondage and the bondage of fear, why, that is a secret.

—ALAN PATON, *Cry, the Beloved Country*

(Dr. Andrew Manson, his wife Christine killed in an accident, has been cleared of charges that he wrongfully removed a patient from a senior colleague to be treated at a tubercular clinic run by a man who was not a physician.)

When their train steamed out Andrew still had an hour to spare. But there was no doubt in his mind as to what he wished to do. Instinctively, he boarded a bus, and soon he was in Kensal Green. He entered the cemetery, stood a long time at Christine's grave, thinking of many things. It was a bright, fresh afternoon, with that crispness in the breeze which she had always loved. Above him, on the branch of a grimy tree, a sparrow chirped merrily.

When at last he turned away, hastening for fear he should be late, there in the sky before him a bank of cloud lay brightly, bearing the shape of battlements.

—A. J. CRONIN, *The Citadel*

(Mrs. Stone, an aging actress, has one last sad affair with a gigolo in Rome.)

. . . It was happening under her direction, for it was she that had made the sign with the white handkerchief, raised it and lowered it quickly in the night air, and then wrapped in it a pair of heavy iron keys which gave admission to the palazzo. And down there, now, the solitary figure, which alone had not seemed to drift while she was helplessly drifting, had moved from its station beneath the Egyptian obelisk and had stooped to pick up the white parcel on the pavement. It looked up at her, the figure, with a single quick jerk of the head, and even now it was moving out of sight, not away from her but toward her. It was disappearing, no, it had already disappeared beneath the cornice that covered the door to the palazzo, and in a little while now, yes, in a few minutes now, the nothingness would be interrupted, the awful vacancy would be entered by something.

Mrs. Stone looked up at the sky which gave her the impression of having suddenly paused. She smiled to herself, and whispered, *Look! I've stopped the drift!*

—TENNESSEE WILLIAMS, *The Roman Spring of Mrs. Stone*

. . . If, at least, there were granted me time enough to complete my work, I would not fail to stamp it with the seal of that Time the understanding of which was this day so forcibly impressing itself upon me, and I would therein describe men—even should that give them the semblance of monstrous creatures—as occupying in Time a place far more considerable than the so restricted one allotted them in space, a place, on the contrary, extending boundlessly since, giant-like, reaching far back into the years, they touch simultaneously epochs of their lives—with countless intervening

days between—so widely separated from one another in
Time.

—MARCEL PROUST, *Remembrance of Things Past*
[*The Past Recaptured*],
trans. Frederick A. Blossom

4 ❀ Unhappily Ever After

magine the opera *Otello* ending with a love duet instead of a murder, the Moor having accepted Desdemona's avowal of innocence. Or a *Rigoletto* in which the jester's daughter Gilda, stabbed and dying in her father's arms, miraculously recovers. Or a *Carmen* in which the gypsy girl is allowed to survive to a tempestuous old age.

In the nineteenth century, Italian opera was performed with just such conclusions, last scenes that seem inconceivable to us now. In fact, composers were under great pressure to write the *lieto fine*, or happy ending, in which good was rewarded, fate and circumstance laughed at, and only the villain destroyed. Audiences of the time demanded these artistic compromises; in England, too, Shakespearean tragedies were rewritten to end happily. Yet it is interesting that *Otello*, *Rigoletto*, and *Carmen*—and the Shakespeare plays—have survived as we know them, with the sacrifice of innocence and goodness to passion and vengeance, and all the cathartic qualities of true tragedy.

One reason for this is undoubtedly that tragedy is simply more dramatic. Any television news show is proof of that. But another is that in its own way, the unhappy ending can be as satisfying as the happy ending. It is an acceptable denouement to an unlikely relationship or a situation that even the author cannot imagine continuing. Especially during and following the Victorian period, it was a way to justify the portrayal of an "immoral" hero: Hardy's Tess, driven to murdering the man who has ruined her, must hang; Flaubert's Emma Bovary, desperately grasping at happiness in adulterous affairs, must take poison; Conrad's Lord Jim, having once abandoned the passengers on a doomed pilgrim ship, must atone for his cowardice in seeking an honorable death.

Endings like these that conclude with the hero's death allow the author, having entangled the hero irreparably, to resolve those entanglements cleanly and dramatically. In fact, death comes almost as a relief to the life the hero has been leading, even as a moral victory and a triumph. If the hero is spared the ultimate punishment of death, he must at least atone for his fall from grace and vow to live a purer existence. Few heroes are permitted to get away, literally or figuratively, with murder.

Of course, the hero must be a hero in the classical sense: not too perfect but not too evil, noble but with a tragic flaw. We can accept a tragic ending because of the catharsis we experience, that is: we have identified with the hero, suffered with him, pitied him, felt awe as he stood against Fate or catastrophe, exulted as he changed or grew, and triumphed with him as he upheld his ideals even unto death. *La commedia è finita*, our emotions have been totally spent, our souls cleansed, and contrary to what we would expect at such an unhappy outcome, we are not angry or depressed, but elated.

Although death is the consummate unhappy ending, it is not the only one. The separation of lovers, the destruction of a self-consuming ambition, the prospect of a lonely old age—all leave the characters and vicariously, the reader, sadder but wiser. We shall look at death in another chapter, but first, here are selections from novels that end in less finite "unhappily ever afters."

La Commedia È Finita ⌐

The hero's trials are mercifully at an end.

Upon the cornice of the tower a tall staff was fixed. Their eyes were riveted on it. A few minutes after the hour had struck something moved slowly up the staff, and extended itself upon the breeze. It was a black flag.

"Justice" was done, and the President of the Immortals (in Æschylean phrase) had ended his sport with Tess. And the D'Urberville knights and dames slept on in their tombs unknowing. The two speechless gazers bent themselves down to the earth, as if in prayer, and remained thus a long time, absolutely motionless: the flag continued to wave silently. As soon as they had strength they arose, joined hands again, and went on.

—THOMAS HARDY, *Tess of the D'Urbervilles*

(Kit Sorrell, who has become a doctor through his father's lifelong labor and sacrifice, hastens the death of the terminally ill man.)
Kit went to the window, and while he was standing there a long pause came in the flow of his father's breathing. Kit's own breathing seemed to pause with it. Again, it was resumed, but very gently, and with a rustling and pathetic serenity. Life was passing, and all the pain and the stress were passing with it.

The window grew more grey. Kit could distinguish the branches and the foliage of the old pear tree black against the gradual dawn. And suddenly, he turned quickly and looked towards the bed. His father's breathing had ceased; he saw the dim face on the pillow. The stillness held.

Kit turned again to the window where the grey world was coming to life before eyes that were wet and blurred.

—WARWICK DEEPING, *Sorrell and Son*

(Paul Morel and his sister have ended their mother's suffering from cancer by putting an overdose of morphine in her milk, and, distraught at losing her, Morel is tempted to kill himself.)
. . . Where was he?—one tiny upright speck of flesh, less than an ear of wheat lost in the field. He could not bear it. On every side the immense dark silence seemed pressing

him, so tiny a spark, into extinction, and yet, almost nothing, he could not be extinct. Night, in which everything was lost, went reaching out, beyond stars and sun. Stars and sun, a few bright grains, went spinning round for terror, and holding each other in embrace, there in a darkness that outpassed them all, and left them tiny and daunted. So much, and himself, infinitesimal, at the core a nothingness, and yet not nothing.

"Mother!" he whimpered—"mother!"

She was the only thing that held him up, himself, amid all this. And she was gone, intermingled herself. He wanted her to touch him, have him alongside with her.

But no, he would not give in. Turning sharply, he walked towards the city's gold phosphorescence. His fists were shut, his mouth set fast. He would not take that direction, to the darkness, to follow her. He walked towards the faintly humming, glowing town, quickly.

—D. H. LAWRENCE, *Sons and Lovers*

(Frederic Henry, an American who had fallen in love with an English nurse while an ambulance driver in Italy during World War I, loses her and their son in childbirth in a Swiss hospital. The doctor tries to help.)

"Good-night," he said. "I cannot take you to your hotel?"

"No, thank you."

"It was the only thing to do," he said. "The operation proved—"

"I do not want to talk about it," I said.

"I would like to take you to your hotel."

"No, thank you."

He went down the hall. I went to the door of the room.

"You can't come in now," one of the nurses said.

"Yes I can," I said.

"You can't come in yet."

"You get out," I said. "The other one too."

But after I had got them out and shut the door and turned off the light it wasn't any good. It was like saying good-by to a statue. After a while I went out and left the hospital and walked back to the hotel in the rain.

—ERNEST HEMINGWAY, *A Farewell to Arms*

(The peak of the volcano, Popocatepetl, rises above the bar from which Mexican villagers throw the alcoholic British ex-consul, Geoffrey Firmin, to his death.)

. . . Strong hands lifted him. Opening his eyes, he looked down, expecting to see, below him, the magnificent jungle, the heights, Pico de Orizabe, Malinche, Cofre de Perote, like those peaks of his life conquered one after another before this greatest ascent of all had been successfully, if unconventionally, completed. But there was nothing there: no peaks, no life, no climb. Nor was this summit a summit exactly: it had no substance, no firm base. It was crumbling too, whatever it was, collapsing, while he was falling, falling into the volcano, he must have climbed it after all, though now there was this noise of foisting lava in his ears, horribly, it was in eruption, yet no, it wasn't the volcano, the world itself was bursting, bursting into black spouts of villages catapulted into space, with himself falling through it all, through the inconceivable pandemonium of a million tanks, through the blazing of ten million burning bodies, falling, into a forest, falling—

Suddenly he screamed, and it was as though this scream were being tossed from one tree to another, as its echoes returned, then, as though the trees themselves were crowding nearer, huddled together, closing over him, pitying . . .

Somebody threw a dead dog after him down the ravine.

—MALCOLM LOWRY, *Under the Volcano*

(Mrs. Moresby, rescued from her ordeal in the Moroccan desert, is delivered to a hotel in Marrakesh. Crazed, she is momentarily left alone in the cab.)

A few minutes later two men walked out to the waiting cab. They looked inside, glanced up and down the sidewalk; then they spoke questioningly to the driver, who shrugged his shoulders. At that moment a crowded streetcar was passing by, filled largely with native dock workers in blue overalls. Inside it the dim lights flickered, the standees swayed. Rounding the corner and clanging its bell, it started up the hill past the Café d'Eckmühl-Noiseux where the awnings flapped in the evening breeze, past the Bar Métropole with its radio that roared, past the Café de France, shining with mirrors and brass. Noisily it pushed along, cleaving a passage through the crowd that filled the street, it scraped around another corner, and began the slow ascent of the Avenue

Galliéni. Below, the harbor lights came into view and were distorted in the gently moving water. Then the shabbier buildings loomed, the streets were dimmer. At the edge of the Arab quarter the car, still loaded with people, made a wide U-turn and stopped; it was the end of the line.

—PAUL BOWLES, *The Sheltering Sky*

(Jolyon Forsyte goes to console the wife of his cousin Soames, Irene, whose lover has been killed in the London fog.)
The visitor turned. It was young Jolyon.

"The door was open," he said. "Might I see your wife for a minute, I have a message for her?"

Soames gave him a strange, sidelong stare.

"My wife can see no one," he muttered doggedly.

Young Jolyon answered gently: "I shouldn't keep her a minute." Soames brushed by him and barred the way.

"She can see no one," he said again.

Young Jolyon's glance shot past him into the hall, and Soames turned. There in the drawing-room doorway stood Irene, her eyes were wild and eager, her lips were parted, her hands outstretched. In the sight of both men that light vanished from her face; her hands dropped to her sides; she stood like stone.

Soames spun round, and met his visitor's eyes, and at the look he saw in them, a sound like a snarl escaped him. He drew his lips back in the ghost of a smile.

"This is my house," he said; "I manage my own affairs.

I've told you once—I tell you again; we are not at home."
And in young Jolyon's face he slammed the door.

—JOHN GALSWORTHY, *The Forsyte Saga*
[The Man of Property]

There were still some miles to ride before they reached the next village, and Abélard and Héloïse rode immersed in the sad belief that their lives were wasted and that their last hope was heaven. Abélard believed in heaven, therefore Héloïse believed, and, united at last, they rode to Troyes, thinking how they were to live out the few years that remained for them to live, thereby gaining an immortal happiness, the letters germinating in their minds as they rode, hints of them appearing in their talk as mile after mile went by.

But it would be vain indeed to record their lives and their talk further, for the rest of their lives and their speech are on record.

—GEORGE MOORE, *Héloïse and Abélard*

(Agreeing to throw a baseball play-off game, then striking out in the last inning after he had changed his mind, Roy Hobbs is revolted at himself, despite having returned the bribery money.)
At the corner near some stores he watched the comings and goings of the night traffic. He felt the insides of him beginning to take off (chug chug choo choo . . .). Pretty soon they were in fast flight. A boy thrust a newspaper at him. He wanted to say no but had no voice. The headline screamed,

"Suspicion of Hobbs's Sellout—Max Mercy." Under this was a photo Mercy had triumphantly discovered, showing Roy on his back, an obscene bullet imbedded in his gut. Around him danced a naked lady: "Hobbs at nineteen."

And there was also a statement by the baseball commissioner. "If this alleged report is true, that is the last of Roy Hobbs in organized baseball. He will be excluded from the game and all his records forever destroyed."

Roy handed the paper back to the kid.

"Say it ain't true, Roy."

When Roy looked into the boy's eyes he wanted to say it wasn't but couldn't, and he lifted his hands to his face and wept many bitter tears.

—BERNARD MALAMUD, *The Natural*

Each night, for many weeks thereafter, Frith came to the lighthouse and fed the pinioned birds. Then one early morning a German pilot on a dawn raid mistook the old abandoned light for an active military objective, dived onto it, a screaming steel hawk, and blew it and all it contained into oblivion.

That evening when Fritha came, the sea had moved in through the breached walls and covered it over. Nothing was left to break the utter desolation. No marsh fowl had dared to return. Only the frightless gulls wheeled and soared and mewed their plaint over the place where it had been.

—PAUL GALLICO, *The Snow Goose*

(Rushing to return to their Cornwall estate, Manderley, which the mysterious housekeeper, Mrs. Danvers, has suddenly left, the de Winters find it, and the specter of Rebecca, in flames.)

"Maxim," I said. "Maxim, what is it?"

He drove faster, much faster. We topped the hill before us and saw Lanyon lying in a hollow at our feet. There to the left of us was the silver streak of the river, widening to the estuary at Kerrith six miles away. The road to Manderley lay ahead. There was no moon. The sky above our heads was inky black. But the sky on the horizon was not dark at all. It was shot with crimson, like a splash of blood. And the ashes blew towards us with the salt wind from the sea.

—DAPHNE DU MAURIER, *Rebecca*

Paradise Lost ⌒

Things will never be the same.

(Wandering out into the snow, Gerald Crich has frozen to death in the Alps. Ursula tries to understand her husband's obsession with his dead friend.)

"Did you need Gerald?" she asked one evening.

"Yes," he said.

"Aren't I enough for you?" she asked.

"No," he said. "You are enough for me, as far as a woman is concerned. You are all women to me. But I wanted a man friend, as eternal as you and I are eternal."

"Why aren't I enough?" she said. "You are enough for me.

I don't want anybody else but you. Why isn't it the same with you?"

"Having you, I can live all my life without anybody else, any other sheer intimacy. But to make it complete, really happy, I wanted eternal union with a man too: another kind of love," he said.

"I don't believe it," she said. "It's an obstinacy, a theory, a perversity."

"Well—" he said.

"You can't have two kinds of love. Why should you!"

"It seems as if I can't," he said. "Yet I wanted it."

"You can't have it, because it's false, impossible," she said.

"I don't believe that," he answered.

—D. H. LAWRENCE, Women in Love

(Clive, frightened of being ruined by the scandal of a homosexual relationship, has abandoned Maurice and married Anne.)
. . . His last words were "Next Wednesday, say at 7:45. Dinner-jacket's enough, as you know."

They were his last words, because Maurice had disappeared thereabouts, leaving no trace of his presence except a little pile of the petals of the evening primrose, which mourned from the ground like an expiring fire. To the end of his life Clive was not sure of the exact moment of departure, and with the approach of old age he grew uncertain whether the moment had yet occurred. The Blue Room would glimmer, ferns undulate. Out of some external Cambridge his friend began beckoning to him, clothed in the sun, and shaking out the scents and sounds of the May term.

But at the time he was merely offended at a discourtesy, and compared it with similar lapses in the past. He did not realize that this was the end, without twilight or compromise, that he should never cross Maurice's track again, nor speak to those who had seen him. He waited for a little in the alley, then returned to the house, to correct his proofs and to devise some method of concealing the truth from Anne.

—E. M. FORSTER, *Maurice*

(Kate Croy has encouraged her lover, Merton Denscher, to pretend love for the rich and terminally ill Millie Theale in hopes of being left her money. When Millie does die, he finds he cannot take the money and marry Kate.)

"You must choose."

Strange it was for him then that she stood in his own rooms doing it, while, with an intensity now beyond any that had ever made his breath come slow to him, he waited for her act. "There's but one thing that can save you from my choice."

"From your choice of my surrender to you?"

"Yes"—and she gave a nod at the long envelope on the table—"your surrender of that."

"What is it then?"

"Your word of honour that you're not in love with her memory."

"Oh—her memory!"

"Ah"—she made a high gesture—"don't speak of it as if you couldn't be. *I* could, in your place; and you're one for whom it will do. Her memory's your love. You *want* no other."

He heard her out in stillness, watching her face, but not moving. Then he only said: "I'll marry you, mind you, in an hour."

"As we were?"

"As we were."

But she turned to the door, and her headshake was now the end. "We shall never be again as we were!"

—HENRY JAMES, *The Wings of the Dove*

(Jennie watches a train bear the body of her reconciled lover, Lester Kane—whom she had nursed in his last days—to the woman he married to retain his inheritance.)

Jennie stood rigid, staring into the wonder of this picture, her face white, her eyes wide, her hands unconsciously clasped, but one thought in her mind—they were taking his body away. A leaden November sky was ahead, almost dark. She looked, and looked until the last glimmer of the red lamp on the receding sleeper disappeared in the maze of smoke and haze overhanging the tracks of the far-stretching yard.

"Yes," said the voice of a passing stranger, gay with the anticipation of coming pleasures. "We're going to have a great time down there. Remember Annie? Uncle Jim is coming and Aunt Ella."

Jennie did not hear that or anything else of the chatter and bustle around her. Before her was stretching a vista of lonely years down which she was steadily gazing. Now what? She was not so old yet. There were those two orphan children to raise. They would marry and leave after a while, and then what? Days and days in endless reiteration, and then—?

—THEODORE DREISER, *Jennie Gerhardt*

(Abandoned by fortune-hunting Morris Townsend because of her threatened disinheritance, the heiress Catherine Sloper has the grim satisfaction of rejecting him when he returns at the urging of her aunt after the death of Catherine's father.)

"That was a precious plan of yours!" said Morris, clapping on his hat.

"Is she so hard?" asked Mrs. Penniman.

"She doesn't care a button for me—with her confounded little dry manner."

"Was it very dry?" pursued Mrs. Penniman, with solicitude.

Morris took no notice of her question; he stood musing an instant, with his hat on. "But why the deuce, then, would she never marry?"

"Yes—why indeed?" sighed Mrs. Penniman. And then, as if from a sense of the inadequacy of this explanation, "But you will not despair—you will come back?"

"Come back? Damnation!" And Morris Townsend strode out of the house, leaving Mrs. Penniman staring.

Catherine, meanwhile, in the parlor, picking up her

morsel of fancy-work, had seated herself with it again—for
life, as it were.

—HENRY JAMES, Washington Square

*(Lady Brett Ashley, who, while waiting for her divorce, had fallen
unhappily in love with Jake Barnes, an American correspondent
emasculated by a war wound, is leaving Madrid to return to the
man she was planning to marry once she was free.)*
Down-stairs we came out through the first-floor dining-
room to the street. A waiter went for a taxi. It was hot and
bright. Up the street was a little square with trees and grass
where there were taxis parked. A taxi came up the street, the
waiter hanging out at the side. I tipped him and told the
driver where to drive, and got in beside Brett. The driver
started up the street. I settled back. Brett moved close to me.
We sat close against each other. I put my arm around her and
she rested against me comfortably. It was very hot and
bright, and the houses looked sharply white. We turned out
onto the Gran Via.

"Oh, Jake," Brett said, "we could have had such a damned
good time together."

Ahead was a mounted policeman in khaki directing traffic.
He raised his baton. The car slowed suddenly pressing Brett
against me.

"Yes," I said. "Isn't it pretty to think so?"

—ERNEST HEMINGWAY, The Sun Also Rises

(Isabel Osmond, rejecting the sexual attraction and promise of independence offered by Caspar Goodwood, follows her conscience and flees to London and a friend, then Rome. There, she returns to her unhappy marriage, her duty and obligations, and is thus forged through suffering into a lady.)

"Pray what led you to suppose she was here?"

"I went down to Gardencourt this morning, and the servant told me she had come to London. He believed she was to come to you."

Again Miss Stackpole held him—with an intention of perfect kindness—in suspense.

"She came here yesterday, and spent the night. But this morning she started for Rome."

Caspar Goodwood was not looking at her; his eyes were fastened on the doorstep.

"Oh, she started—" he stammered. And without finishing his phrase, or looking up, he turned away.

Henrietta had come out, closing the door behind her, and now she put out her hand and grasped his arm.

"Look here, Mr. Goodwood," she said; "just you wait!"

On which he looked up at her*—but only to guess, from her face, with a revulsion, that she simply meant he was young. She stood shining at him with that cheap comfort, and it added, on the spot, thirty years to his life. She walked him away with her, however, as if she had given him now the key to patience.

—HENRY JAMES, *The Portrait of a Lady*

*The novel originally ended here. James added what follows to the New York edition to clarify the intention of the ending.

(Impersonating the King of Ruritania for three months, Rudolf Rassendyll falls in love with the Queen-to-be, Flavia, who sacrifices their happiness for the sake of duty.)

Shall I see her face again—the pale face and the glorious hair? Of that I know nothing; Fate has no hint, my heart no presentiment. I do not know. In this world, perhaps—nay, it is likely—never. And can it be that somewhere, in a manner whereof our flesh-bound minds have no apprehension, she and I will be together again, with nothing to come between us, nothing to forbid our love? That I know not, nor wiser heads than mine. But if it be never—if I can never hold sweet converse again with her, or look upon her face, or know from her her love, why, then, this side the grave, I will live as becomes the man whom she loves; and for the other side I must pray a dreamless sleep.

—ANTHONY HOPE, *The Prisoner of Zenda*

(Maria tearfully tells Porgy that Bess has been taken off to Savannah in Porgy's absence, in an ending with none of the hope of the Gershwin opera, Porgy and Bess.*)*

Deep sobs stopped Maria's voice. For a while she sat there, her face buried in her hands. But Porgy had nothing to say. When she finally raised her head and looked at him, she was surprised at what she saw.

The keen autumn sun flooded boldly through the entrance and bathed the drooping form of the goat, the ridiculous wagon, and the bent figure of the man in hard, satirical radiance. In its revealing light, Maria saw that Porgy was an old man. The early tension that had characterized him, the mellow mood that he had known for one eventful summer, both had gone; and in their place she saw a face that sagged wearily, and the eyes of age lit only by a faint reminiscent glow from suns and moons that had looked into them, and had already dropped down the west.

She looked until she could bear the sight no longer; then she stumbled into her shop and closed the door, leaving Porgy and the goat alone in an irony of morning sunlight.

—DU BOSE HEYWARD, *Porgy*

(Clara, mad after her son Swan has killed her husband and then himself, is visited by her stepson in the nursing home where she will spend the rest of her life.)

She was quieter than usual the rest of that day. She sat with her hands in her lap, still and silent and grieved. When Clark tried to talk with her she did not seem to hear him. Looking at her, he felt his throat ache with a grief of his own—his wife did not understand what this grief was, why he drove so far to visit this woman, and he could not explain it to her. He was to keep coming for the rest of Clara's life, for many years, though she would sometimes not bother to look away from her television set when he appeared.

She seemed to like best programs that showed men fighting, swinging from ropes, shooting guns and driving fast cars, killing the enemy again and again until the dying gasps of evil men were only a certain familiar rhythm away from the

opening blasts of the commercials, which changed only
gradually over the years.

—JOYCE CAROL OATES, A Garden of Earthly Delights

And as I sat there brooding on the old, unknown world, I
thought of Gatsby's wonder when he first picked out the
green light at the end of Daisy's dock. He had come a long
way to this blue lawn, and his dream must have seemed so
close that he could hardly fail to grasp it. He did not know
that it was already behind him, somewhere back in that vast
obscurity beyond the city, where the dark fields of the
republic rolled on under the night.

Gatsby believed in the green light, the orgiastic future that
year by year recedes before us. It eluded us then, but that's
no matter—tomorrow we will run faster, stretch out our
arms farther. . . . And one fine morning—

So we beat on, boats against the current, borne back
ceaselessly into the past.

—F. SCOTT FITZGERALD, The Great Gatsby

5 ❀ THE DEAD END

s birth is a natural beginning to a novel, death is a natural end. Whether it is the hero who dies or a person beloved or hated by the hero, this last action is often the climactic event of the book. I use the term "climax" not in the theatrical sense, where it is an action by the protagonist that can occur near the middle of the play—for example, Hamlet's killing of Polonius, after which Hamlet moves inexorably toward the unhappy resolution of the play—but as that point toward which the story has been building, and where the action really ends.

In many, perhaps most, cases the death pivotal to the plot occurs in the penultimate chapter, the last being saved to show the effect that the event has on the major character or characters. This chapter is an anticlimax or what might be more accurately called a postclimax: the forward movement of the story has been halted at the point of highest tension, and the last chapter is only a period of cooling down and reflection. Thus John Galsworthy describes the death of the honest but pitiable Soames Forsyte in the next-to-last chapter of *Swan Song*, the final book of *The Forsyte Saga*. His daughter, Fleur, waits with him for the doctor:

> "Gradman is here, darling, and Mother, and Aunt Winifred, and Kit and Michael. Is there anyone you would like to see?"
>
> His lips shaped: "No—you!"
>
> "I am here all the time." Again she felt the tremor from his fingers, saw his lips whispering:
>
> "That's all."
>
> And suddenly, his eyes went out. There was nothing there! For some time longer he breathed, but before "that fellow" came, he had lost hold—was gone.

Galsworthy uses the last chapter to establish the ultimate effect of the death. Through the eyes of Soames's son-in-law, Michael Mont, we see that the marriage of Michael and Fleur will survive Soames's death and Fleur's infidelity.

Killing off a character as strong as Soames is not an easy undertaking, as Sir Arthur Conan Doyle found when he attempted to do away with Sherlock Holmes. The outcry from readers was so great that, much to the annoyance of his creator, the character had to be brought back in another book. There was to be no such miraculous reappearance for Soames once Galsworthy had decided on his death. Nearing the completion of *Swan Song*, Galsworthy wrote to a friend that he thought Soames would "survive" the book, but four months later he confided that he had finished the novel and "after all 'Le Roi est mort'—" It was a not insignificant decision for Galsworthy or his readers.

The Harder They Fall ⌐
Deaths of the great and near-great.

He continued to murmur, to move his hands a little, and Magdalena thought he was trying to ask for something, or to tell them something. But in reality the Bishop was not there at all; he was standing in a tip-tilted green field among his native mountains, and he was trying to give consolation to a young man who was being torn in two before his eyes by the desire to go and the necessity to stay. He was trying to forge a new Will in that devout and exhausted priest; and the time was short, for the *diligence* for Paris was already rumbling down the mountain gorge.

When the Cathedral bell tolled just after dark, the Mexican population of Santa Fé fell upon their knees, and all American Catholics as well. Many others who did not kneel prayed in their hearts. Eusabio and the Tesuque boys went quietly away to tell their people; and the next morning the old Archbishop lay before the high altar in the church he had built.

—WILLA CATHER, *Death Comes for the Archbishop*

The second page of a letter from John Galsworthy to Harley Granville-Barker, August 12, 1927, revealing that the author had "killed" his character, Soames Forsyte, in the final book of *The Forsyte Saga*: "after all 'Le Roi est mort—'" *(Houghton Library, Harvard University, bMS Eng 1020 [39])*

(Theo van Gogh witnesses his brother Vincent's burial.)
The attendants lowered the coffin into the ground. Then they shovelled in dirt and stamped it down.

The seven men turned, left the cemetery, and walked down the hill.

Doctor Gachet returned a few days later to plant sunflowers all about the grave.

Theo went home to the Cité Pigalle. His loss pushed out every aching second of the night and day with unassuagable grief.

His mind broke under the strain.

Johanna took him to the *maison de santé* in Utrecht, where Margot had gone before him.

At the end of six months, almost to the day of Vincent's death, Theo passed away. He was buried at Utrecht.

Some time later, when Johanna was reading her Bible for comfort, she came across the line in Samuel:

And in their death they were not divided.

She took Theo's body to Auvers, and had it placed by the side of his brother.

When the hot Auvers sun beats down upon the little cemetery in the cornfields, Theo rests comfortably in the luxuriant umbrage of Vincent's sunflowers.

—IRVING STONE, *Lust for Life*

(Libanius has been forbidden by the Emperor to publish Julian's biography.)

I have been reading Plotinus all evening. He has the power to soothe me; and I find his sadness curiously comforting. Even when he writes: "Life here with the things of earth is a sinking, a defeat, a failing of the wing." The wing has indeed failed. One sinks. Defeat is certain. Even as I write these lines, the lamp wick sputters to an end, and the pool of light in which I sit contracts. Soon the room will be dark. One has always feared that death would be like this. But what else is there? With Julian, the light went, and now nothing remains but to let the darkness come, and hope for a new sun and another day, born of time's mystery and man's love of light.

—GORE VIDAL, *Julian*

(Alexander has died, and is guarded by Bagoas, his eunuch slave and lover, as soldiers break into the bedchamber.)

. . . There were shouts and hammerings; those outside broke in the doors. Perdikkas and Ptolemy called to their men to defend the King's body from traitors and pretenders. I was almost crushed as they backed around the bed. The wars for the world had started; these people were fighting to possess him, as if he were a thing, a symbol, like the Mitra or the throne. I turned to him. When I saw him still lie calm, bearing all this without resentment, then I knew he was truly dead.

They had begun to fight, and were throwing javelins. I

stood to shield him, and one of them grazed my arm. I have the scar to this day, the only wound I ever took for him.

Presently they parleyed, and went away to go on with their dispute outside. I bound up my arm with a bit of towel, and waited, for it was not proper he should be without attendance. I lit the night-lamp and set it by the bed, and watched with him, till at morning the embalmers came to take him from me, and fill him with everlasting myrrh.

—MARY RENAULT, *The Persian Boy*

(From Suetonius: The Lives of the Caesars: *Book One.)*
. . . As Caesar exclaimed: "Then this is violence!" one of the Cascas, standing at his side, plunged a dagger into him, just below the throat. Caesar caught hold of Casca's arm and ran his pen through it; but as he tried to rise to his feet he was held down by another stab. When he saw that he was surrounded on all sides by drawn daggers, he wrapped his head in his robe at the same time drawing its folds about his feet with his left hand so that when he fell the lower part of his body would be decorously covered.

In this manner then he was stabbed twenty-three times. He said no word, merely groaned at the first stroke, though certain writers have said that when Marcus Brutus fell upon him he said in Greek, "You, too, my son!"

All the conspirators took themselves off and left him lying there dead for some time. Finally three common slaves put him on a litter and carried him home, one arm hanging down over the side.

Antistius the physician said that of all those wounds only the second one in the breast would have proved fatal.

—THORNTON WILDER, *The Ides of March*

At that moment the tramp of a horse was heard. That was the centurion coming with soldiers for the head of Ahenobarbus.

"Hurry!" cried the freedmen.

Nero placed the knife to his neck, but pushed it only timidly. It was clear that he would never have the courage to thrust it in. Epaphroditus pushed his hand suddenly,—the knife sank to the handle. Nero's eyes turned in his head, terrible, immense, frightened.

"I bring thee life!" cried the centurion, entering.

"Too late!" said Nero, with a hoarse voice; then he added,— "Here is faithfulness!"

In a twinkle death seized his head. Blood from his heavy neck gushed in a dark stream on the flowers of the garden. His legs kicked the ground, and he died.

On the morrow the faithful Acte wrapped his body in costly stuffs, and burned him on a pile filled with perfumes.

And so Nero passed, as a whirlwind, as a storm, as a fire, as war or death passes; but the basilica of Peter rules till now, from the Vatican heights, the city, and the world.

Near the ancient Porta Capena stands to this day a little chapel with the inscription, somewhat worn: *Quo Vadis, Domine?*

—HENRYK SIENKIEWICZ, *Quo Vadis,*
trans. Jeremiah Curtin

(General Simón Bolívar, forced from power, realizes that he is dying.)

"Damn it," he sighed. "How will I ever get out of this labyrinth!"

He examined the room with the clairvoyance of his last days, and for the first time he saw the truth: the final borrowed bed, the pitiful dressing table whose clouded, patient mirror would not reflect his image again, the chipped porcelain washbasin with the water and towel and soap meant for other hands, the heartless speed of the octagonal clock racing toward the ineluctable appointment at seven minutes past one on his final afternoon of December 17. Then he crossed his arms over his chest and began to listen to the radiant voices of the slaves singing the six o'clock *Salve* in the mills, and through the window he saw the diamond of Venus in the sky that was dying forever, the eternal snows, the new vine whose yellow bellflowers he would not see bloom on the following Saturday in the house closed in mourning, the final brilliance of life that would never, through all eternity, be repeated again.

—GABRIEL GARCÍA MÁRQUEZ,
The General in His Labyrinth,
trans. Edith Grossman

Murder Most Foul ⌐

Death comes violently.

(An Autobahn patrolman finds James Bond and his new bride, whose Lancia has crashed after having been shot at from a Maserati.)
Bond turned towards Tracy. She was lying forward with her face buried in the ruins of the steering-wheel. Her pink handkerchief had come off and the bell of golden hair hung down and hid her face. Bond put his arm round her shoulders, across which the dark patches had begun to flower.

He pressed her against him. He looked up at the young man and smiled his reassurance.

"It's all right," he said in a clear voice as if explaining something to a child. "It's quite all right. She's having a rest. We'll be going on soon. There's no hurry. You see"—Bond's head sank down against hers and he whispered into her hair—"you see, we've got all the time in the world."

The young patrolman took a last scared look at the motionless couple, hurried over to his motor-cycle, picked up the hand-microphone and began talking urgently to the rescue headquarters.

—IAN FLEMING, *On Her Majesty's Secret Service*

(The Captain goes to the room of his wife, whom he suspects of infidelity, to find crouching at the side of the bed a soldier who had been stealing into her room as she slept.)
The soldier did not have time to rise from his squatting position. He blinked at the light and there was no fear in his

face; his expression was one of dazed annoyance, as if he had been inexcusably disturbed. The Captain was a good marksman, and although he shot twice only one raw hole was left in the center of the soldier's chest.

The reports from the pistol aroused Leonora and she sat up in bed. As yet she was still only half-awake, and she stared about her as though witnessing some scene in a play, some tragedy that was gruesome but not necessary to believe. Almost immediately Major Langdon knocked on the back door and then hurried up the stairs wearing slippers and a dressing-gown. The Captain had slumped against the wall. In his queer, coarse wrapper he resembled a broken and dissipated monk. Even in death the body of the soldier still had the look of warm, animal comfort. His grave face was unchanged, and his sun-browned hands lay palms upward on the carpet as though in sleep.

—CARSON MCCULLERS, *Reflections in a Golden Eye*

(The ship's officer, Ryuji, is to be murdered by a group of young boys for deserting the sea to live on land and to marry the mother of one of them, Noboru.)

. . . Surging out of the splendor of the sea, death had swept down on him like a stormy bank of clouds. A vision of death now eternally beyond his reach, majestic, acclaimed, heroic death unfurled its rapture across his brain. And if the world had been provided for just this radiant death, then why shouldn't the world also perish for it!

Waves, as tepid as blood, inside an atoll. The tropical sun

blaring across the sky like the call of a brass trumpet. The many-colored sea. Sharks. . . .

Another step or two and Ryuji would have regretted it.

"Here's your tea," Noboru offered from behind him, thrusting a dark-brown plastic cup near Ryuji's cheek. Absently, Ryuji took it. He noticed Noboru's hand trembling slightly, probably from the cold.

Still immersed in his dream, he drank down the tepid tea. It tasted bitter. Glory, as anyone knows, is bitter stuff.

—YUKIO MISHIMA,
The Sailor Who Fell from Grace with the Sea,
trans. John Nathan

(At the end of his operational career, Alec Leamas and the woman he loves attempt an escape over the Berlin Wall.)
Then they fired—single rounds, three or four, and he felt her shudder. Her thin arms slipped from his hands. He heard a voice in English from the Western side of the wall:

"Jump, Alec! Jump, man!"

Now everyone was shouting, English, French and German mixed; he heard Smiley's voice from quite close:

"The girl, where's the girl?"

Shielding his eyes he looked down at the foot of the wall and at last he managed to see her, lying still. For a moment he hesitated, then quite slowly he climbed back down the same rungs, until he was standing beside her. She was dead; her face was turned away, her black hair drawn across her cheek as if to protect her from the rain.

They seemed to hesitate before firing again; someone shouted an order, and still no one fired. Finally they shot him, two or three shots. He stood glaring around him like a blinded bull in the arena. As he fell, Leamas saw a small car smashed between great lorries, and the children waving cheerfully through the window.

—JOHN LE CARRÉ,
The Spy Who Came in from the Cold

(Fighting in the Loyalist Army in the Spanish Civil War, Robert Jordan lies wounded, waiting with the last of his strength to kill a Fascist leader.)

As the officer came trotting now on the trail of the horses of the band he would pass twenty yards below where Robert Jordan lay. At that distance there would be no problem. The officer was Lieutenant Berrendo. He had come up from La Granja when they had been ordered up after the first report of the attack on the lower post. They had ridden hard and had then had to swing back, because the bridge had been blown, to cross the gorge high above and come around through the timber. Their horses were wet and blown and they had to be urged into the trot.

Lieutenant Berrendo, watching the trail, came riding up, his thin face serious and grave. His submachine gun lay across his saddle in the crook of his left arm. Robert Jordan lay behind the tree, holding onto himself very carefully and delicately to keep his hands steady. He was waiting until the officer reached the sunlit place where the first trees of the pine forest joined the green slope of the meadow. He could feel his heart beating against the pine needle floor of the forest.

—ERNEST HEMINGWAY, *For Whom the Bell Tolls*

(Ernst Graeber, a German soldier, frees the Russian prisoners he is guarding, as the Russians advance.)
He saw the Russians. They were running bent over in a group with the women in front. One of the men looked back and saw him. All at once the Russian had a rifle in his hand. He lifted it and took aim. Graeber saw the black hole of the muzzle, it grew, he wanted to call out, in a loud voice, there was so much to say quickly and loudly—

He did not feel the shot. He only saw grass suddenly in front of him, a plant, close before his eyes, half trodden down, with a cluster of reddish stalks and delicate, narrow leaves that grew larger, and he had seen this before, but he no longer knew when. The plant wavered and then stood alone against the narrowed horizon of his sinking head, silent, self-evident, with the solace of the tidiness of tiny things and with all its peace; it grew larger and larger until it filled the whole sky, and his eyes closed.

—ERICH MARIA REMARQUE,
A Time to Love and a Time to Die,
trans. Denver Lindley

(Nicolas Salmanovitch Rubashov, a loyal Communist imprisoned on charges of plotting against the State, has been hit on the back of the head.)

. . . He lay crumpled up on the ground, with his cheek on the cool flagstones. It got dark, the sea carried him rocking on its nocturnal surface. Memories passed through him, like streaks of mist over the water.

Outside, someone was knocking on the front door, he dreamed that they were coming to arrest him; but in what country was he?

He made an effort to slip his arm into his dressing-gown sleeve. But whose colour-print portrait was hanging over his bed and looking at him?

Was it No. 1 or was it the other—he with the ironic smile or he with the glassy gaze?

A shapeless figure bent over him, he smelt the fresh leather of the revolver belt; but what insignia did the figure wear on the sleeves and shoulder-straps of its uniform—and in whose name did it raise the dark pistol barrel?

A second, smashing blow hit him on the ear. Then all became quiet. There was the sea again with its sounds. A wave slowly lifted him up. It came from afar and travelled sedately on, a shrug of eternity.

—ARTHUR KOESTLER, *Darkness at Noon,*
trans. Daphne Hardy

(Joseph K., without being told the crime of which he has been accused, is interrogated, released, then taken into custody, marched to a quarry, and executed.)

With a flicker as of a light going up, the casements of a window there suddenly flew open; a human figure, faint and insubstantial at that distance and that height, leaned abruptly far forward and stretched both arms still farther. Who was it? A friend? A good man? Someone who sympathized? Someone who wanted to help? Was it one person only? Or was it mankind? Was help at hand? Were there arguments in his favor that had been overlooked? Of course there must be. Logic is doubtless unshakable, but it cannot withstand a man who wants to go on living. Where was the Judge whom he had never seen? Where was the High Court, to which he had never penetrated? He raised his hands and spread out all his fingers.

But the hands of one of the partners were already at K.'s throat, while the other thrust the knife deep into his heart and turned it there twice. With failing eyes K. could still see the two of them immediately before him, cheek leaning against cheek, watching the final act. "Like a dog!" he said; it was as if the shame of it must outlive him.

—FRANZ KAFKA, *The Trial,*
trans. Willa and Edward Muir,
revised by E. M. Butler

Suicidal Tendencies ⌒
The hero writes his own ending.

(As the effects of worldwide atomic bombing reach Australia, Moira Davidson faces a slow radioactive death while Dwight Towers takes his life in the American submarine he will sink.)

Presently she could see the submarine no longer; it had vanished in the mist. She looked at her little wrist watch; it showed one minute past ten. Her childhood religion came back to her in those last minutes; one ought to do something about that, she thought. A little alcoholically she murmured the Lord's Prayer.

Then she took out the red carton from her bag, and opened the vial, and held the tablets in her hand. Another spasm shook her, and she smiled faintly. "Foxed you this time," she said.

She took the cork out of the bottle. It was ten past ten. She said earnestly, "Dwight, if you're on your way already, wait for me."

Then she put the tablets in her mouth and swallowed them down with a mouthful of brandy, sitting behind the wheel of her big car.

—NEVIL SHUTE, *On the Beach*

He raised his eyes, looked through the kitchen window, saw the immense Greek coping of the library, the huge words cut in granite, Harry Elkins Widener Library, then beyond it the slate roof of Boylston Hall, and farther still the gray wooden steeple of the Unitarian Church. There was a faint smell of coffee coming from the professor's apartment, it mixed oddly with the not unpleasant smell of the gas, he was aware that he was hungry.

But also he was sleepy, it would be very easy to fall asleep. By this time, Jones would have got back to the shabby little house in Reservoir Street—the grave at Mount Auburn would have been filled—the khaki-clad messenger was sitting in a subway train on his way to Beacon Hill. And Gerta— would she be there? would she come? was she standing there at her open window, with an apple in her hand, looking down over the roofs to the morning sunlight flashing on the Charles River Basin? wearing the white Russian blouse?

Half past nine. The professor's clock sent its soft *tyang* through the walls. He closed his eyes.

—CONRAD AIKEN, *King Coffin*

This balcony clings to the living cliff. I see a walk beyond it, threading the crag. That will do well. If I go from here, it might be said that Lykomedes murdered me. It would be discourteous to shame my host. But there is only Akamas left to ask my blood-price; and he, though he is half Cretan, knows well enough how the Erechthids die.

Surely goats made this track. That boy, Achilles, might scramble here for a dare. No place, this, for a dragging foot; but all the better. It will seem like mischance, except to those who know.

The tide comes in. A swelling sea, calm, strong and shining. To swim under the moon, onward and onward, plunging with the dolphins, singing . . . To leap with the wind in my hair . . .

—MARY RENAULT, *The Bull from the Sea*

That evening the swarm of helicopters that came buzzing across the Hog's Back was a dark cloud ten kilometres long. The description of last night's orgy of atonement had been in all the papers.

"Savage!" called the first arrivals, as they alighted from their machine. "Mr. Savage!"

There was no answer.

The door of the lighthouse was ajar. They pushed it open and walked into a shuttered twilight. Through an archway on the further side of the room they could see the bottom of the staircase that led up to the higher floors. Just under the crown of the arch dangled a pair of feet.

"Mr. Savage!"

Slowly, very slowly, like two unhurried compass needles, the feet turned towards the right; north, north-east, east, south-east, south, south-south-west; then paused, and, after a few seconds, turned as unhurriedly back towards the left. South-south-west, south, south-east, east. . . .

—ALDOUS HUXLEY, *Brave New World*

Go Gently ⌒
Death as letting go.

(Adam's wise Chinese servant, Lee, urges the dying man to forgive his son, Caleb, for causing the death of his brother, Aron, who ran away to the war. He gives his blessing with a Hebrew word meaning "thou mayest.")

A terrible brightness shone in Adam's eyes and he closed them and kept them closed. A wrinkle formed between his brows.

Lee said, "Help him, Adam—help him. Give him his chance. Let him be free. That's all a man has over the beasts. Free him! Bless him!"

The whole bed seemed to shake under the concentration. Adam's breath came quick with his effort and then, slowly, his right hand lifted—lifted an inch and then fell back.

Lee's face was haggard. He moved to the head of the bed and wiped the sick man's damp face with the edge of the sheet. He looked down at the closed eyes. Lee whispered, "Thank you, Adam—thank you, my friend. Can you move your lips? Make your lips form his name."

Adam looked up with sick weariness. His lips parted and failed and tried again. Then his lungs filled. He expelled the air and his lips combed the rushing sigh. His whispered word seemed to hang in the air:

"*Timshel!*"

His eyes closed and he slept.

—JOHN STEINBECK, *East of Eden*

He seemed to be choking.

"Mother, it's getting dark," he called feebly.

He gasped. There was a rattle in his throat. He turned livid, his eyes dilated widely, became blank, and he went limp. And in the mind of Studs Lonigan, through an all-increasing blackness, streaks of white light filtered weakly and recessively like an electric light slowly going out. And there was nothing in the mind of Studs Lonigan but this feeble streaking of light in an all-encompassing blackness, and then, nothing.

And by his bedside was a kneeling mother, sobbing and praying, two sisters crying, a brother with his head lowered hiding a solemn and penitent face, a father sick and hurt, and an impatient nurse.

Lonigan went to the kitchen. He poured himself the remains of a bottle of whisky and gulped it. He sat by the table, his face blank, his mouth hanging open. He heard his wife scream.

The two daughters led the hysterical mother out of the room, and the nurse covered the face of Studs Lonigan with a white sheet.

—JAMES T. FARRELL,
Studs Lonigan [Judgment Day]

(Philip Ashley, suspecting that the woman who married his cousin has poisoned both her late husband and himself, does not warn her about an unfinished bridge as she goes for a walk in the garden.)
I came to the edge of the wall above the sunken garden and

saw where the men had started work upon the bridge. Part of the bridge still remained and hung suspended, grotesque and horrible, like a swinging ladder. The rest had fallen to the depths below.

I climbed down to where she lay amongst the timber and the stones. I took her hands and held them. They were cold.

"Rachel," I said to her, and "Rachel" once again.

The dogs began barking up above, and louder still came the sound of the clanging bell. She opened her eyes and looked at me. At first, I think, in pain. Then in bewilderment. Then finally, so I thought, in recognition. Yet I was in error, even then. She called me Ambrose. I went on holding her hands until she died.

They used to hang men at Four Turnings in the old days. Not any more, though.

—DAPHNE DU MAURIER, *My Cousin Rachel*

(George Apley writes to his son John about his own funeral arrangements and the boy's return and entrance into Boston society.)
But I am getting very far afield. I am speaking very prosily, out of sheer joy at having you come back. We can talk about all these matters together much more sensibly than I can ever put them down on paper. My mind and my heart are both too full for writing. I repeat I always knew that you had the right stuff in you and now we will have a chance to get to know each other. What I want particularly is to have a great

many small men's dinners. There is so much to say. There is so much to talk about. God bless you. . . .

George Apley died in his own house on Beacon Street on the thirteenth of December, 1933, two weeks after John Apley returned to Boston.

—JOHN MARQUAND, *The Late George Apley*

From his expression and the pitch of his voice, the boy is shouting into a fierce wind blowing from his father's direction. "Don't *die*, Dad, *don't!*" he cries, then sits back with that question still on his face, and his dark wet eyes shining like stars of a sort. Harry shouldn't leave the question hanging like that, the boy depends on him.

"Well, Nelson," he says, "all I can tell you is, it isn't so bad." Rabbit thinks he should maybe say more, the kid looks wildly expectant, but enough. Maybe. Enough.

—JOHN UPDIKE, *Rabbit at Rest*

. . . "And the pain?" he asked himself. "What has become of it? Where are you, pain?"

He turned his attention to it.

"Yes, here it is. Well, what of it? Let the pain be."

"And death . . . where is it?"

He sought his former accustomed fear of death and did not find it. "Where is it? What death?" There was no fear because there was no death.

In place of death there was light.

"So that's what it is!" he suddenly exclaimed aloud.
"What joy!"

To him all this happened in a single instant, and the meaning of that instant did not change. For those present his agony continued for another two hours. Something rattled in his throat, his emaciated body twitched, then the gasping and rattle became less and less frequent.

"It is finished!" said someone near him.

He heard these words and repeated them in his soul.

"Death is finished," he said to himself. "It is no more!"

He drew in a breath, stopped in the midst of a sigh, stretched out, and died.

—COUNT LEO TOLSTOY, *The Death of Iván Ilých*,
trans. Louise and Aylmer Maude

. . . The thin cold knife separates the tissues. And they find that liquid in your abdominal cavity, and inflamed twists of intestine swollen and tied to your mesentery, swollen hard, full of blood. They find the area of gangrene bathed in fetid liquid. Infart, they say, and repeat: mesenteric infart. They look at your dilated intestine, deep scarlet, almost black. They say: pulse, respiration, temperature, punctiform perforation. Eaten away, corroded. Hemorrhagic fluid drips out of your open belly. Hopeless, they say, hopeless, they repeat. The three. The clot breaks loose. Black blood is thrown out. The blood will flow and then it will stop. It stopped. Your silence and open eyes, sightless eyes. Your icy unfeeling fingers. Your blue-black fingernails. Your quivering jaw.

Artemio Cruz . . . Name . . . hopeless . . . heart massage . . .
hopeless . . . You will not know now. I carry you inside and
with you I die. The three, we . . . will die. You . . . die, have
died . . . I will die.

—CARLOS FUENTES, *The Death of Artemio Cruz*,
trans. Sam Hileman

*(Zorba's death in a small village in Serbia is related in a letter by
the schoolmaster: Zorba has declared he wants no last rites, and says
that men like him "ought to live a thousand years. Good night!")*
These were his last words. He then sat up in his bed, threw
back the sheets and tried to get up. We ran to prevent him—
Lyuba, his wife, and I, along with several sturdy neighbors.
But he brushed us all roughly aside, jumped out of bed and
went to the window. There, he gripped the frame, looked out
far into the mountains, opened wide his eyes and began to
laugh, then to whinny like a horse. It was thus, standing, with
his nails dug into the window frame, that death came to him.

His wife Lyuba asked me to write to you and send her
respects. The deceased often talked about you, she says, and
left instructions that a *santuri* of his should be given to you
after his death to help you to remember him.

The widow begs you, therefore, if you ever pass through
our village, to be good enough to spend the night in her
house as her guest, and when you leave in the morning, to
take the *santuri* with you.

—NIKOS KAZANTZAKIS,
Zorba the Greek, trans. Carl Wildman

Last Words ↩

A final good-bye to the dead.

Coming thus near to the summit of one of the high mountains of the Jura, in the middle of the night, in that little cave magnificently illuminated with countless candles, a score of priests celebrated the Office of the Dead. All the inhabitants of the little mountain villages, through which the procession passed, had followed it, drawn by the singularity of this strange ceremony.

Mathilde appeared in their midst in a flowing garb of mourning, and, at the end of the service, had several thousands of five franc pieces scattered among them.

Left alone with Fouqué, she insisted upon burying her lover's head with her own hands. Fouqué almost went mad with grief.

By Mathilde's orders, this savage grot was adorned with marbles sculptured at great cost, in Italy.

Madame de Rênal was faithful to her promise. She did not seek in any way to take her own life; but, three days after Julien, died while embracing her children.

> —STENDHAL, *The Red and the Black,*
> trans. C. K. Scott Moncrieff

(Sammler speaks to the body of his nephew Elya, which is lying on a stretcher in the hospital morgue.)
Sammler in a mental whisper said, "Well, Elya. Well, well, Elya." And then in the same way he said, "Remember, God,

the soul of Elya Gruner, who, as willingly as possible and as well as he was able, and even to an intolerable point, and even in suffocation and even as death was coming was eager, even childishly perhaps (may I be forgiven for this), even with a certain servility, to do what was required of him. At his best this man was much kinder than at my very best I have ever been or could ever be. He was aware that he must meet, and he did meet—through all the confusion and degraded clowning of this life through which we are speeding—he did meet the terms of his contract. The terms which, in his inmost heart, each man knows. As I know mine. As all know. For that is the truth of it—that we all know, God, that we know, that we know, we know, we know."

—SAUL BELLOW, *Mr. Sammler's Planet*

He saw that all the conditions of life had conspired to keep them apart; since his very detachment from the external influences which swayed her had increased his spiritual fastidiousness, and made it more difficult for him to live and love uncritically. But at least he *had* loved her—had been willing to stake his future on his faith in her—and if the moment had been fated to pass from them before they could seize it, he saw now that, for both, it had been saved whole out of the ruin of their lives.

It was this moment of love, this fleeting victory over themselves, which had kept them from atrophy and extinction; which, in her, had reached out to him in every struggle against the influence of her surroundings, and in him, had kept alive the faith that now drew him penitent and reconciled to her side.

He knelt by the bed and bent over her, draining their last moment to its lees; and in the silence there passed between them the word which made all clear.

—EDITH WHARTON, *The House of Mirth*

(Hazel Motes's landlady, because she herself is losing her sight, doesn't realize that her blinded tenant is dead.)
She had never observed his face more composed and she grabbed his hand and held it to her heart. It was resistless and dry. The outline of a skull was plain under his skin and the deep burned eye sockets seemed to lead into the dark tunnel where he had disappeared. She leaned closer and closer to his face, looking deep into them, trying to see how she had been cheated or what had cheated her, but she couldn't see anything. She shut her eyes and saw the pin point of light but so far away that she could not hold it steady in her mind. She felt as if she were blocked at the entrance of something. She sat staring with her eyes shut, into his eyes, and felt as if she had finally got to the beginnng of something she couldn't begin, and she saw him moving farther and farther away, farther and farther into the darkness until he was the pin point of light.

—FLANNERY O'CONNOR, *Wise Blood*

They rolled him onto the stretcher and carried him to the ambulance. Smoke got in and sat beside him on a jump seat. They drove slowly between streets, but they put on a little speed at intersections and went across with the siren wide open.

The sun was in Rick's face. Smoke reached up and pulled down the blind. Then he settled back and said, "I knew a guy once that took a cure and he said . . . " But he stopped it there because he suddenly knew that it wasn't getting over. He looked down and saw Rick's face. He watched, stunned, and while he was watching, Rick died. He could tell when it happened. There was a difference.

—DOROTHY BAKER, *Young Man with a Horn*

Post-Mortem ⤺

The survivors struggle with their memories.

(Preceding a mob from the ranch on which they are workers, George finds and kills his companion, the simpleminded Lennie, who has accidentally murdered the wife of the boss's son, Curley.)
Slim came directly to George and sat down beside him, sat very close to him. "Never you mind," said Slim. "A guy got to sometimes."

But Carlson was standing over George. "How'd you do it?" he asked.

"I just done it," George said tiredly.

"Did he have my gun?"

"Yeah. He had your gun."

"An' you got it away from him and you took it an' you killed him?"

"Yeah. Tha's how." George's voice was almost a whisper. He looked steadily at his right hand that had held the gun.

Slim twitched George's elbow. "Come on, George. Me an' you'll go in an' get a drink."

George let himself be helped to his feet. "Yeah, a drink."

Slim said, "You hadda, George. I swear you hadda. Come on with me." He led George into the entrance of the trail and up toward the highway.

Curley and Carlson looked after them. And Carlson said, "Now what the hell ya suppose is eatin' them two guys?"

—JOHN STEINBECK, *Of Mice and Men*

(Danny has died, and his house is accidentally set on fire; his friends let it burn so no stranger can have it.)

The sirens screamed from Monterey. The trucks roared up the hill in second gear. The searchlights played among the trees. When the Department arrived, the house was one great blunt spear of flame. The hoses wet the trees and brush to keep the flames from spreading.

Among the crowding people of Tortilla Flat, Danny's friends stood entranced and watched until at last the house was a mound of black, steaming cinders. Then the fire trucks turned and coasted away down the hill.

The people of the Flat melted into the darkness. Danny's friends still stood looking at the smoking ruin. They looked at one another strangely, and then back to the burned house.

And after a while they turned and walked slowly away, and no two walked together.

—JOHN STEINBECK, *Tortilla Flat*

"Oliver," he said, "you should have told me."

It was very cold, which in a way was good because I was numb and wanted to feel *something*. My father continued to address me, and I continued to stand still and let the cold wind slap my face.

"As soon as I found out, I jumped into the car."

I had forgotten my coat; the chill was starting to make me ache. Good. Good.

"Oliver," said my father urgently, "I want to help."

"Jenny's dead," I told him.

"I'm sorry," he said in a stunned whisper.

Not knowing why, I repeated what I had long ago learned from the beautiful girl now dead.

"Love means not ever having to say you're sorry."

And then I did what I had never done in his presence, much less in his arms. I cried.

—ERICH SEGAL, *Love Story*

The Bolter came to see me while I was still in the Oxford nursing home where my baby had been born and where Linda had died.

"Poor Linda," she said, with feeling, "poor little thing. But

Fanny, don't you think perhaps it's just as well? The lives of women like Linda and me are not so much fun when one begins to grow older."

I didn't want to hurt my mother's feelings by protesting that Linda was not that sort of woman.

"But I think she would have been happy with Fabrice," I said. "He was the great love of her life, you know."

"Oh, dulling," said my mother, sadly. "One always thinks that. Every, every time."

—NANCY MITFORD, *The Pursuit of Love*

(Governor Skeffington has died, and his nephew passes his house one last time.)

. . . The cab drove on down the long straight stretch; the house was still visible, and Adam, through the rear window, saw the dark bulk of the big house, and then, suddenly, for just an instant, and through some queer trick of the imagination, it seemed to him that through the dim light and the softly falling evening snow, he could see the ghosts of the lines that had once formed at the door, and now would form no more. And he knew, with one, quick, final ache, that he would miss his uncle very much, in ways he did not yet know, and he knew too, that in missing him, he would never be alone.

The cab swerved around another bend; the house was gone. Slowly Adam turned away from the rear window; to the driver he said: "All right. You can cut over on the next left."

The driver nodded; Adam sat back once more against the cushions, his eyes closed. The pilgrimage, and with it, a part of his life, was over; he was going home.

—EDWIN O'CONNOR, *The Last Hurrah*

(Paris Trout, having killed the fourteen-year-old black girl, Rosie Sayers, his mother, and two townspeople, before killing himself, leaves behind his wife, Hanna.)

In her dreams everything was dark. She could never see the walls or the floor or her own hands. She would stumble, catching herself a moment before she fell, and then stumble again. Always moving toward a voice that called for help.

The tripping frightened her—she remembered there was glass on the floor—but in the dark, at the bottom of things, she always kept on. In her dreams she knew the voice.

And when she woke from that other place, grabbing at the roll of the mattress for some purchase to break her fall, she would hold herself still for as long as the dream was fresh, trying to hear the voice again, but the fear would pass before she could bring it back.

And then it was gone.

And she would lie in the dark until morning sometimes, wondering which one of them it was.

—PETE DEXTER, *Paris Trout*

(Alma Mason, who lives with her brother Boyd, is writing a memorial to their nephew, Cliff.)

"I've thought of Cliff a bit today, Boyd," she said at last, and she felt he nodded. "This was his day."

"You mustn't ever feel he didn't know," she heard his voice coming to her as if out of some eternal darkness. It was Boyd's old confident strong voice before he had got sick. "Cliff knew we cared, Alma," he told her. "And that made him care too, at last, though he maybe never said it, and he didn't have the gift, you and I know, to write it."

There was no answer.

"Did you hear what I said?" Boyd asked. "Sometimes I think your hearing is nearly as bad as mine." He could only see her nod, not hear her voice.

By their practice of sitting in the dark, only their white hair which at times shone almost like phosphorescence betokened each other's presence.

Through the open windows there came the faint delicious perfume of azaleas. The court house clock struck ten.

—JAMES PURDY, The Nephew

(Mrs. Hale relates how Ethan and Mattie, crippled for life from a lovers' suicide attempt, must depend on Ethan's harping wife to care for them.)

She took off her spectacles again, leaned toward me across the bead-work table-cover, and went on with lowered voice: "There was one day, about a week after the accident, when they all thought Mattie couldn't live. Well, I say it's a pity she *did.* I said it right out to our minister once, and he was shocked at me. Only he wasn't with me that morning when she first came to . . . And I say, if she'd ha' died, Ethan might ha' lived; and the way they are now, I don't see's there's much difference between the Fromes up at the farm and the Fromes down in the graveyard; 'cept that down there they're all quiet, and the women have got to hold their tongues."

—EDITH WHARTON, Ethan Frome

When the short funeral procession started, Mary and the infirm Fossette (sole relic of the connection between the Baines family and Paris) were left alone in the house. The tearful servant prepared the dog's dinner and laid it before her in the customary soup-plate in the customary corner. Fossette sniffed at it, and then walked away and lay down with a dog's sigh in front of the kitchen fire. She had been deranged in her habits that day; she was conscious of neglect, due to events which passed her comprehension. And she did not like it. She was hurt, and her appetite was hurt. However, after a few minutes, she began to reconsider the matter. She glanced at the soup-plate, and, on the chance that it might after all contain something worth inspection, she awkwardly balanced herself on her old legs and went to it again.

—ARNOLD BENNETT, The Old Wives' Tale

(Don Fabrizio's spinster daughter, Concetta, whose only love, Tancredi, has died, disposes of her dead father's possessions, including his stuffed dog.)

Still she could feel nothing; the inner emptiness was complete; but she did sense an unpleasant atmosphere exhaling from the heap of furs. That was to-day's distress: even poor Bendicò was hinting at bitter memories. She rang the bell. "Annetta," she said, "This dog has really become too moth-eaten and dusty. Take it out and throw it away."

As the carcass was dragged off, the glass eyes stared at her with the humble reproach of things that are thrown away, got rid of. A few minutes later what remained of Bendicò was flung into a corner of the courtyard visited every day by the dustman. During the flight down from the window its form recomposed itself for an instant; in the air there seemed to be dancing a quadruped with long whiskers, its right foreleg raised in imprecation. Then all found peace in a heap of livid dust.

—GIUSEPPE DI LAMPEDUSA, *The Leopard,*
trans. Archibald Colquhoun

(Unaware that her son has died, Francesca Bassington's brother informs her that one of the possessions she had valued even above the boy is not genuine.)

"My dear Francesca," he said soothingly, laying his hand affectionately on her arm, "I know that this must be a great disappointment to you, you've always set such store by this picture, but you mustn't take it too much to heart. These disagreeable discoveries come at times to most picture fanciers and owners. Why, about twenty per cent. of the alleged Old Masters in the Louvre are supposed to be wrongly attributed. And there are heaps of similar cases in this country. Lady Dovecourt was telling me the other day that they simply daren't have an expert in to examine the Van Dykes at Columbey for fear of unwelcome disclosures. And, besides, your picture is such an excellent copy that it's by no means without a value of its own. You must get over the disappointment you naturally feel, and take a philosophical view of the matter. . . ."

Francesca sat in stricken silence, crushing the folded morsel of paper tightly in her hand and wondering if the thin, cheerful voice with its pitiless, ghastly mockery of consolation would never stop.

—SAKI, *The Unbearable Bassington*

6 ❈ IRONY—WITH A TWIST, PLEASE

hat extraordinary power the novelist holds over us as he or she brings the story to a close! The author can make us laugh or cry, can inspire us with hope or make us ache with despair. Or toy with us, telling us one thing when really something very different is meant, and playing with our emotions so that we react first one way then another. The novelist can, in other words, choose to give the ending an ironic twist.

We should know better. If we were alert, we would see that early in the story we are being set up by being given little clues that will eventually lead to the "trick" ending. But if the novelist is doing the job cleverly, we will accept these clues for what they seem to be: details of character or plot that only take on a greater meaning when we view the whole story with the benefit of that seventh sense, hindsight.

At that point, irony delivers an emotional whammy.

The dramatic power inherent in this effect is the reason irony is such a popular ending with playwrights and television and screenwriters, where it is commonly called the "twist." A very contemporary ending, it's as old as the ancient Greeks, from whom it originated. In fact, one form of irony, in which a feigned innocent statement is used to prove an opponent wrong, is called Socratic irony.

Scholars have identified many different ironic forms: verbal, including the use of sarcasm, in which the dialogue contains the contradiction; dramatic, which is brought about by a situation or fateful series of events that lead to the exact opposite result from that expected by the protagonist and which gives us our greatest tragedies; comic, which hurts us even as we laugh; the irony of character, in which the character himself gives the lie to our, and sometimes his, expectations, an un-unveiled Tartuffe; and many others, such as symbolic, recurring, malignant, benevolent, and subconscious irony. Although they function somewhat differently, all are based on a single principle: deception. And the deceiver is the author, pretending one thing and meaning its opposite, acting on the characters as it sometimes seems Fate acts on us in real life, unreasonably, heartlessly and with supreme fickleness.

Our reaction to the ironic ending is twofold: intellectually we recognize that what we see is not what it is purported to be, and we appreciate the cleverness with which we have been taken in; and emotionally we feel some hurt, or at least discomfort, in perceiving the truth. We get the joke, but we do not wholly like it. It is like black comedy where, in the middle of a laugh, we gasp in horror at its implications.

The author can achieve a similar emotional impact through ironic understatement, that is, by seemingly leaving out what is most important. The author ends the book with a coolness and distance, and we as readers, realizing what has been left unsaid, fill in the blanks. So, John Fowles's narrator in *The Collector*, having slowly killed the young woman he has kept imprisoned in a room in his house, buries the body and considers preparing the room for a new victim, concluding: "But it is still just an idea. I only put the stove down there today because the room needs drying out anyway." What seems an innocent observation by the "collector" makes our skin crawl as we realize the author's implication.

How Ironic! ⇝
The author has a last wry smile at our expense.

(Madame Bovary is dead from arsenic obtained from the pharmacist; her husband, Charles, dies disillusioned and in poverty.)
When everything was sold, there remained twelve francs and fifteen centimes—enough to pay Mademoiselle Bovary's coach fare to her grandmother's. The old lady died the same year; and since Monsieur Rouault was now paralyzed, it was an aunt who took charge of her. She is poor, and sends her to work for her living in a cotton mill.

Since Bovary's death, three doctors have succeeded one another in Yonville, and not one of them has gained a foothold, so rapidly and so utterly has Homais routed them. The devil himself doesn't have a greater following than the pharmacist: the authorities treat him considerately, and public opinion is on his side.

He has just been awarded the cross of the Legion of Honor.

—GUSTAVE FLAUBERT, *Madame Bovary,*
trans. Francis Steegmuller

The church thundered with the triumphant hallelujah, and in a sacred silence Elmer prayed:

"O Lord, thou hast stooped from thy mighty throne and rescued thy servant from the assault of the mercenaries of Satan! Mostly we thank thee because thus we can go on doing thy work, and thine alone! Not less but more zealously shall we seek utter purity and the prayer-life, and rejoice in freedom from all temptations!"

He turned to include the choir, and for the first time he saw that there was a new singer, a girl with charming ankles and lively eyes, with whom he would certainly have to become well acquainted. But the thought was so swift that it did not interrupt the pæan of his prayer:

"Let me count this day, Lord, as the beginning of a new and more vigorous life, as the beginning of a crusade for complete morality and the domination of the Christian church through all the land. Dear Lord, thy work is but begun! We shall yet make these United States a moral nation!"

—SINCLAIR LEWIS, *Elmer Gantry*

(Laura Rowan has just agreed to leave London and her English family to return to Russia with her Russian mother, Tania.)
". . . And when all our peasants understand the new ways of farming, and all these new factories and railways are working, and all the men who are liberal like your uncles—you will like your uncles—have forced the Tsar to grant a constitution, nobody'll be poor, nobody will be oppressed. And all over the world the old stupidities are going to die. I don't believe there'll be another war after this wretched South African business, we've all too much to lose. And people are getting so clever, there's science, it's going to do wonderful things, indeed, it's doing them already." She threw back her head and laughed as if she knew a wonderful secret. "Think of it, in ten and twenty years, with this radium treatment, nobody will ever die of cancer. Oh, my darling, unhappiness has touched us, but you are young, you are going to live in a happy, happy age."

There was a knock on the door, and they delayed only long enough to smile at each other, and to exchange a kiss.
—REBECCA WEST, *The Birds Fall Down*

(Brian Tate is to be reconciled with his wife, Erica, after his affair with a young student.)
They will talk for a long while after lunch, Brian imagines. Moving into the sitting room—Erica curled on the blue sofa as usual, and he in his wing chair—they will relate and explain all that has passed. They will laugh, and possibly at some moments cry. They will encourage each other, console

each other, and forgive each other. Finally, as the afternoon lengthens and the shadows of half-fledged trees reach toward the house, they will put their arms about each other and forget for a few moments that they were once exceptionally handsome, intelligent, righteous and successful young people; they will forget that they are ugly, foolish, guilty and dying.

More and more marchers are crowding into the park now. A group of mothers and small children has just come up to the fountain. One young woman leans over the basin beside Brian to wet a folded diaper and wipe the red-stained sticky face of a toddler in a stroller, while a boy just slightly older jerks the sleeve of her sweater to get her attention.

"Mommy?" he asks. "Mommy, will the war end now?"
—ALISON LURIE, *The War Between the Tates*

(Karen Holmes is leaving Hawaii for home, after Pearl Harbor and her extramarital love affair with Sergeant Milton Warden.)
She took the six flower leis off over her head and dropped them over the side. This was as good a place to drop them over as any. Diamond Head, Koko Head, Makapuu Head. Perhaps Koko Head was the best place, really. The six leis fell together and the wind blew them back against the side of the ship and out of sight and she did not see them light on the water.

"Mother," her son said from behind her. "I'm hungry. When do we eat on this old boat?"

"Pretty soon now," she said.

"Mother, do you think the war will last long enough so I can graduate from the Point and be in it? Jerry Wilcox said it wouldnt."

"No," she said, "I dont think it'll last that long."

"Well, gee whiz, mother," her son said, "I want to be in it."

"Well, cheer up," Karen said, "and dont let it worry you. You may miss this one, but you'll be just the right age for the next one."

"You really think so, mother?" her son said anxiously.

—JAMES JONES, *From Here to Eternity*

(Ed Gentry has survived a three-day canoe trip on a wild part of a river in the South, during which he and three friends were viciously attacked by mountain men, one of whom they killed; the area has since been developed.)

Though Lake Cahula hasn't built up like the one we're on, there are indications that people are getting interested in it, as they always do any time a new, nice place opens up in what the real estate people call an unspoiled location. I expect there are still a few deer around Lake Cahula—deer that used to spend most of their time on the high ground at the top of the gorge—but in a few years they will be gone, and perhaps only the unkillable tribe of rabbits will be left. One big marina is already built on the south end of the lake, and my wife's younger brother says that the area is beginning to catch on, especially with the new generation, the one just getting out of high school.

—JAMES DICKEY, *Deliverance*

(The scheming Bel-Ami has just married the daughter of his lover, while another mistress, Mme. de Marelle, has intimated that their affair will continue as before.)

When they reached the threshold he saw a crowd gathered outside, come to gaze at him, Georges du Roy. The people of Paris envied him. Raising his eyes, he saw beyond the Place de la Concorde, the chamber of deputies, and it seemed to him that it was only a stone's throw from the portico of the Madeleine to that of the Palais Bourbon.

Leisurely they descended the steps between two rows of spectators, but Georges did not see them; his thoughts had returned to the past, and before his eyes, dazzled by the bright sunlight, floated the image of Mme. de Marelle, rearranging the curly locks upon her temples before the mirror in their apartments.

—GUY DE MAUPASSANT, *Bel-Ami*

So this was the end! From his protestant upbringing Augustine knew that what once a convent has swallowed it never gives up . . .

Flinging his things into the old Gladstone bag that had once been his father's he could hardly see what he was doing: he was more like a boxer practising on a punch-bag than a young man packing his clothes.

Where was he going to next? Anywhere anywhere anywhere! Over the frontier to whatever other country was nearest! But then, as he turned again to the wardrobe his bag called after him: "You don't know when you're lucky!"

Augustine turned round in surprise; but he was wrong, it was only a bag.

—RICHARD HUGHES, *The Fox in the Attic*

(James Bray, an English colonial administrator who had been expelled from his post in Africa ten years before for supporting local nationalist leaders, returns and is killed.)

No one could say for certain whether, when Bray was killed on the way to the capital, he was going to Mweta or to buy arms for Shinza. To some, as his friend Dando had predicted, he was a martyr to savages; to others, one of those madmen like Geoffrey Bing or Conor Cruise O'Brien who had only got what he deserved. In a number devoted to "The Decline of Liberalism" in an English monthly journal he was discussed as an interesting case in point: a man who had "passed over from the scepticism and resignation of empirical liberalism to become one of those who are so haunted by the stupidities and evils in human affairs that they are prepared to accept apocalyptic solutions, wade through blood if need be, to bring real change."

Hjalmar Wentz also put together Bray's box of papers and gave them over to Dando, who might know what to do with them. Eventually they must have reached the hands of Mweta. He, apparently, chose to believe that Bray was a conciliator; a year later he published a blueprint for the country's new education scheme, the Bray Report.

—NADINE GORDIMER, *A Guest of Honour*

(Captain Chris Baldry is a war victim of amnesia who has resumed a relationship with an innkeeper's daughter because he cannot remember his wife, Kitty. His cousin Jenny watches as he is told the truth by the woman, who sacrifices their happiness for Kitty's.)

. . . He wore a dreadful decent smile; I knew how his voice would resolutely lift in greeting us. He walked not loose limbed like a boy, as he had done that very afternoon, but with the soldier's hard tread upon the heel. It recalled to me that, bad as we were, we were yet not the worst circumstance of his return. When we had lifted the yoke of our embraces from his shoulders he would go back to that flooded trench in Flanders under that sky more full of flying death than clouds, to that No Man's Land where bullets fall like rain on the rotting faces of the dead. . . .

"Jenny, aren't they there?"

"They're both there."

"Is he coming back?"

"He's coming back."

"Jenny, Jenny! How does he look?"

"Oh. . . ." How could I say it? "Every inch a soldier."

She crept behind me to the window, peered over my shoulder and saw.

I heard her suck her breath with satisfaction. "He's cured!" she whispered slowly. "He's cured!"

—REBECCA WEST, *The Return of the Soldier*

That's an Understatement! ⌐◡

The silence speaks volumes.

The room's cleaned out now and good as new.

I shall put what she wrote and her hair up in the loft in the deed-box which will not be opened till my death, so I don't expect for forty or fifty years. I have not made up my mind about Marian (another M! I heard the supervisor call her name), this time it won't be love, it would just be for the interest of the thing and to compare them and also the other thing, which as I say I would like to go into in more detail and I could teach her how. And the clothes would fit. Of course I would make it clear from the start who's boss and what I expect.

But it is still just an idea. I only put the stove down there today because the room needs drying out anyway.

—JOHN FOWLES, *The Collector*

(John Dowell is aware that Edward Ashburnham is about to commit suicide, Ashburnham having just received a telegram from the young girl he loves, whom Leonora, his wife, has connived to banish to India.)

Then he put two fingers into the waistcoat pocket of his grey, frieze suit; they came out with a little neat penknife— quite a small penknife. He said to me:

"You might just take that wire to Leonora." And he looked at me with a direct, challenging, brow-beating glare.

I guess he could see in my eyes that I didn't intend to hinder him. Why should I hinder him?

I didn't think he was wanted in the world, let his confounded tenants, his rifle-associations, his drunkards, reclaimed and unreclaimed, get on as they liked. Not all the hundreds and hundreds of them deserved that that poor devil should go on suffering for their sakes.

When he saw that I did not intend to interfere with him his eyes became soft and almost affectionate. He remarked:

"So long, old man, I must have a bit of a rest, you know."

I didn't know what to say. I wanted to say: "God bless you," for I also am a sentimentalist. But I thought that perhaps that would not be quite English good form, so I trotted off with the telegram to Leonora. She was quite pleased with it.

—FORD MADOX FORD, *The Good Soldier*

(The "gentleman" Miss Goering was to meet has forgotten her and is driving off with three friends.)
He slammed the door behind him and they drove off. Miss Goering began to descend the stone steps. The long staircase seemed short to her, like a dream that is remembered long after it has been dreamed.

She stood on the street and waited to be overcome with joy and relief. But soon she was aware of a new sadness within herself. Hope, she felt, had discarded a childish form forever.

"Certainly I am nearer to becoming a saint," reflected Miss

Goering, "but is it possible that a part of me hidden from my sight is piling sin upon sin as fast as Mrs. Copperfield?" This latter possibility Miss Goering thought to be of considerable interest but of no great importance.

—JANE BOWLES, *Two Serious Ladies*

. . . Arthur already had the bags in the car and on the luggage rack. They shook hands and Arthur left, and Laskell saw him take Micky from Nancy. They all three stood waving at him, Nancy showing Micky how to wave. Laskell waved back. Nancy blew a kiss and showed Micky how to blow a kiss and then the train left.

Laskell put the rod up with the bags and he tried to put the creel up too. The creel was coming back without having held a single fish, but this was not the first time it had done that. The creel would not fit on the rack with the bags, nor would the bowl, so he kept these on the seat beside him.

—LIONEL TRILLING, *The Middle of the Journey*

(Gerald Higgins has written the history of Robert Millhouser, who had killed his wife years before.)
I left him then and I never saw him again. He would not see me, although he sent us handsome presents when Frances and I were married and when our children were born. I was in the Navy when he died, aged eighty-nine. Later I figured out that at the moment of his death I was at my battle station,

and it was entirely possible that as I stared into the darkness above the Leyte Gulf I was thinking of him and the Portuguese shores on the other side of the world. I often tried to think of things like that to take my mind off Frances and the stories that had got back to me.

—JOHN O'HARA, *Ourselves to Know*

I had a terrible idea, it would be good if a person would grow old a bit faster? It seems a long time to wait for that Change of Life I hear about. That's no way for a woman to feel. That shows what it does to you, being by yourself. Listen, snowstorm, you can't do that to me.

I might go over and visit with Delphine, she and Mr Detaille are always home Sundays. There's that memo to the Toilet Goods Association to check over. Besides it's always fun to watch Pfui try to dig his nails into the slippery floor.

Mark said he'd call, but if I got out before the bell rings? He's always hurt if I don't say darling. He says "You don't greet me darling? Is it an argument?"

They must have possibilities or they couldn't be so sensitive.

Well I can say darling without committing myself to nothing. Darling is only politeness nowadays. Dearest is what I couldn't say unless by accident?

I bet that's him now. Jesusgod, what will I tell him.

Hello darling.

—CHRISTOPHER MORLEY, *Kitty Foyle*

Carter called today, but I saw no point in talking to him. On the whole I talk to no one. I concentrate on the way light would strike filled Mason jars on a kitchen windowsill. I lie here in the sunlight, watch the hummingbird. This morning I threw the coins in the swimming pool, and they gleamed and turned in the water in such a way that I was almost moved to read them. I refrained.

One thing in my defense, not that it matters: I know something Carter never knew, or Helene, or maybe you. I know what "nothing" means, and keep on playing.

Why, BZ would say.

Why not, I say.

—JOAN DIDION, *Play It as It Lays*

. . . I have spoken of a voice telling me things. I was getting to know it better now, to understand what it wanted. It did not use the words that Moran had been taught when he was little and that he in his turn had taught to his little one. So that at first I did not know what it wanted. But in the end I understood this language. I understood it, I understood it, all wrong perhaps. That is not what matters. It told me to write the report. Does this mean I am freer now than I was? I do not know. I shall learn. Then I went back into the house and wrote, It is midnight. The rain is beating on the windows. It was not midnight. It was not raining.

—SAMUEL BECKETT, *Molloy,* trans. Patrick Bowles
in collaboration with the author

The others hadn't survived. But he had. He hadn't even died of cancer. And now his exile was cracking like an eggshell.

He remembered the *komendant* advising him to get married. They'd all be giving him advice like that soon.

It was good to lie down. Good.

The train shuddered and moved forward. It was only then that in his heart, or his soul, somewhere in his chest, in the deepest seat of his emotion, he was seized with anguish. He twisted his body and lay face down on his greatcoat, shut his eyes and thrust his face into the duffel bag, spiky with leaves.

The train went on and Kostoglotov's boots dangled toes down over the corridor like a dead man's.

An evil man threw tobacco in the Macaque Rhesus's eyes. Just like that . . .

—ALEXANDER SOLZHENITSYN, *Cancer Ward*, trans. Nicholas Bethell and David Burg

(Effie Perine is shocked at Spade's coldheartedness.)

Her voice was queer as the expression on her face. "You did that, Sam, to her?"

He nodded. "Your Sam's a detective." He looked sharply at her. He put his arm around her waist, his hand on her hip. "She did kill Miles, angel," he said gently, "offhand, like that." He snapped the fingers of his other hand.

She escaped from his arm as if it had hurt her. "Don't, please, don't touch me," she said brokenly. "I know—I know you're right. You're right. But don't touch me now—not now."

Spade's face became pale as his collar.

The corridor-door's knob rattled. Effie Perine turned quickly and went into the outer office, shutting the door behind her. When she came in again she shut it behind her.

She said in a small flat voice: "Iva is here."

Spade, looking down at his desk, nodded almost imperceptibly. "Yes," he said, and shivered. "Well, send her in."

—DASHIELL HAMMETT, *The Maltese Falcon*

Little Georgi, however, behind the mahogany table was revolving a few simple and extremely banal thoughts. Marvelous the life you see in a big hotel like this, he was thinking. Marvelous. Always something going on. One man goes to prison, another gets killed. One leaves, another comes. They carry off one man on a stretcher by the back stairs, and at the same moment another man hears he has a baby. Interesting—if you like! But such is Life!

Dr. Otternschlag sat in the middle of the lounge, a stone image of Loneliness and Death. He has his *en pension* terms, and so he stays on. His yellow hands hang down like lead, and with his glass eye he stares out into the street which is full of sunshine that he cannot see. . . .

The revolving door turns and turns—and swings . . . and swings . . . and swings. . . .

—VICKI BAUM, *Grand Hotel*

". . . and the cooking is getting perfectly disgraceful. I spoke to Culyer about it only yesterday. But he won't do anything.

I don't know what's the good of the committee. This club isn't half what it used to be. In fact, Wimsey, I'm thinking of resigning."

"Oh, don't do that, Wetheridge. It wouldn't be the same place without you."

"Look at all the disturbance there has been lately. Police and reporters—and then Penberthy blowing his brains out in the library. And the coal's all slate. Only yesterday something exploded like a shell—I assure you, exactly like a shell—in the card-room; and as nearly as possible got me in the eye. I said to Culyer, 'This must *not* occur again.' You may laugh, but I knew a man who was blinded by a thing popping out suddenly like that. These things never happened before the War, and—great heavens! William! Look at this wine! Smell it! *Taste* it! Corked? Yes, I should think it *was* corked! My God! I don't know what's come to this club."

—DOROTHY L. SAYERS,
The Unpleasantness at the Bellona Club

7 SURPRISE!

he quintessential surprise ending is the revelation of the murderer in the mystery novel. If the story has been well planned, this surprise will take the reader totally unawares, yet it will be entirely logical and acceptable because of the preparation that has gone before. A track will have been laid and clues given throughout the book, clues that mean little when we first read them but that make absolute sense when the surprise is revealed. "Of course," we say to ourselves, "it was so obvious if only I'd seen."

The same basic rules apply to the surprise ending of a non-mystery novel. Carefully laid clues prepare us for what is to come, and because we accept them as we progress through the book, we accept the author's tricking us at the end. Although the ending appears on the surface to be unexpected, it really *has* been expected all along. When we think about it, two and two *do* make four.

The author has again deceived us, but our reaction to this kind of deception is very different from our response to the ironic ending, which makes us somewhat uncomfortable. With the surprise ending, we are pleased. Pleased that we have been fooled. Pleased with relief from the tension that has been building. Pleased that a solution has appeared as miraculously as the proverbial knight in shining armor.

Yet although the surprise comes magically, it still must make sense to us, based on all we have read previously in the book. If it doesn't, if it is surprise for the sake of surprise, our reaction is not pleasure. It is disbelief and annoyance.

The Hat Trick ⟅

The author pulls out a rabbit.

(Having killed the painter of his portrait, which ages while he doesn't, Dorian Gray stabs the painting, then falls to the floor with a crash and cry.)

Inside, in the servants' part of the house, the half-clad domestics were talking in low whispers to each other. Old Mrs. Leaf was crying and wringing her hands. Francis was as pale as death.

After about a quarter of an hour, he got the coachman and one of the footmen and crept upstairs. They knocked, but there was no reply. They called out. Everything was still. Finally, after vainly trying to force the door, they got on the roof, and dropped down on to the balcony. The windows yielded easily: their bolts were old.

When they entered they found, hanging upon the wall, a splendid portrait of their master as they had last seen him, in all the wonder of his exquisite youth and beauty. Lying on the floor was a dead man, in evening dress, with a knife in his heart. He was withered, wrinkled, and loathsome of visage. It was not till they had examined the rings that they recognised who it was.

— OSCAR WILDE, *The Picture of Dorian Gray*

(The creature, on board ship in the Arctic with the explorer Walton, cries out his remorse to the dead Frankenstein.)
"But soon," he cried, with sad and solemn enthusiasm, "I shall die, and what I now feel be no longer felt. Soon these burning miseries will be extinct. I shall ascend my funeral pile triumphantly, and exult in the agony of the torturing flames. The light of that conflagration will fade away; my ashes will be swept into the sea by the winds. My spirit will sleep in peace; or if it thinks, it will not surely think thus. Farewell."

He sprung from the cabin-window, as he said this, upon the ice-raft which lay close to the vessel. He was soon borne away by the waves and lost in darkness and distance.

— MARY SHELLEY, *Frankenstein*

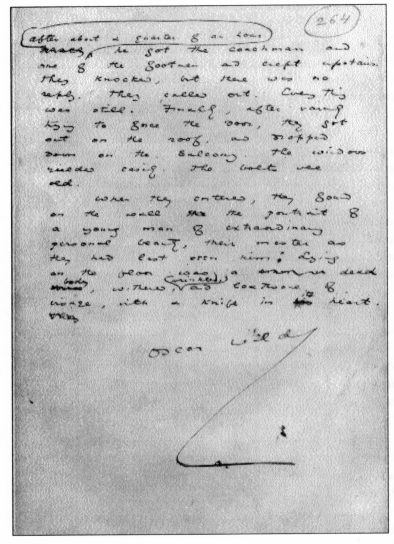

The last page of the original manuscript of Oscar Wilde's *The Picture of Dorian Gray. (The Pierpont Morgan Library, New York, MA 833)*

(Ulysse Mérou returns to Earth with Nova, the beautiful woman he has rescued from Soror, the planet ruled by apes.)

The truck stops fifty yards from us. I pick my son up in my arms and leave the launch. Nova follows us after a moment's hesitation. She looks frightened but she will soon get over it.

The driver gets out of the vehicle. He has his back turned to me. He is half concealed by the long grass growing in the space between us. He opens the door for the passenger to alight. I was not mistaken, he is an officer; a senior officer, as I now see from his badges of rank. He jumps down. He takes a few steps toward us, emerges from the grass, and at last appears in full view. Nova utters a scream, snatches my son from me, and rushes back with him to the launch, while I remain rooted to the spot, unable to move a muscle or utter a sound.

He is a gorilla.

—PIERRE BOULLE, *Planet of the Apes,* trans. Xan Fielding

(Sixty years before, as her pursued lover was about to leave her for the Cause, Lady L. had hidden him in the Madras strongbox in her private retreat.)

"Sometimes I cannot bear it," she said. "I just can't bear the idea that one day I will die and lose you forever. I just can't imagine not coming here to be with you, to sit with you, to talk to you, to live with you as I have done almost every day during the last sixty years."

The Poet Laureate finally managed to speak. But his voice came out strangely high and almost eunuchlike, and even then he couldn't find the words.

"You mean to say that he's still—that you have . . . "

Then his voice failed him again and he just sat there, pointing a shaking finger at the thing.

Lady L. took from her pocket a heavy black key and put it into the lock. She turned it twice and opened the door.

Armand was kneeling there in his gray courtier coat. The white knee breeches and the silk stockings adhered to the bones, or hung limply around them. There was a leather bag—with a black mantilla over it. A pistol lay between the buckled shoes. The right hand of the skeleton held a red tulle rose.

—ROMAIN GARY, *Lady L.*

My God, that bloody casket has fallen on the floor! Some people were hammering in the next flat and it fell off its bracket. The lid has come off and whatever was inside it has certainly got out. Upon the demon-ridden pilgrimage of human life, what next I wonder?

—IRIS MURDOCH, *The Sea, The Sea*

(Miles Coverdale reveals his secret.)

. . . There is one secret,—I have concealed it all along, and never meant to let the least whisper of it escape,—one foolish little secret, which possibly may have had something to do with these inactive years of meridian manhood, with my bachelorship, with the unsatisfied retrospect that I fling back on life, and my listless glance towards the future. Shall I reveal it? It is an absurd thing for a man in his afternoon,—a man of the world, morever, with these three white hairs in his brown mustache and that deepening track of a crow's-foot on each temple,—an absurd thing ever to have happened, and quite the absurdest for an old bachelor, like me, to talk about. But it rises to my throat; so let it come.

I perceive, moreover, that the confession, brief as it shall be, will throw a gleam of light over my behavior throughout the foregoing incidents, and is, indeed, essential to the full understanding of my story. The reader, therefore, since I have disclosed so much, is entitled to this one word more. As I write it, he will charitably suppose me to blush, and turn away my face:—

I—I myself—was in love—with—PRISCILLA!

—NATHANIEL HAWTHORNE, *The Blithedale Romance*

"Goodbye, Yossarian," the chaplain called. "And good luck. I'll stay here and persevere, and we'll meet again when the fighting stops."

"So long, Chaplain. Thanks, Danby."

"How do you feel, Yossarian?"

"Fine. No, I'm very frightened."

"That's good," said Major Danby. "It proves you're still alive. It won't be fun."

Yossarian started out. "Yes it will."

"I mean it, Yossarian. You'll have to keep on your toes every minute of every day. They'll bend heaven and earth to catch you."

"I'll keep on my toes every minute."

"You'll have to jump."

"I'll jump."

"Jump!" Major Danby cried.

Yossarian jumped. Nately's whore was hiding just outside the door. The knife came down, missing him by inches, and he took off.

— JOSEPH HELLER, *Catch-22*

(Ensign Pulver, searching for something to assuage his grief over Mister Roberts's death, turns to the potted palms the Captain obsessively keeps on deck.)

The Captain was sitting, reading, in the large chair of his cabin. In the cone of harsh light from the floor lamp he looked old, and not evil, but merely foolish. He glanced up at the knock on the opened door.

"Yeah," he said gruffly, "what is it?"

Ensign Pulver leaned a casual hand on the door jamb. "Captain," he said easily, "I just threw your damn palm trees over the side."

— THOMAS HEGGEN, *Mister Roberts*

(Visiting Curtin, Howard tells how he is revered by the Indians, who think he has powers as a medicine man.)

"There you see, partner," Howard said to Curtin, "what an important person I am, and I want you to respect me properly."

"I certainly will, señor doctor." Curtin laughed mockingly and shook hands with Howard.

"And hurry up, old boy, and get well."

"I'm feeling fine already. I'm sure I will be okay inside of three days. As soon as I can sit in a saddle, I shall come over to your village to see the great doctor performing his miracles."

Howard had no time to answer, for the Indians snatched him away from his pal, dragged him out, and lifted him on his horse. No sooner was he seated in the saddle than the Indians shouted, whipped their ponies into action, and hurried back home.

—B. Traven, *The Treasure of the Sierra Madre*

Colonel Bishop staggered in, and stood waiting.

At the table sat a man of whom nothing was visible but the top of a carefully curled black head. Then his head was raised, and a pair of blue eyes solemnly regarded the prisoner. Colonel Bishop made a noise in his throat, and, paralyzed by amazement, stared into the face of his excellency the Deputy-Governor of Jamaica, which was the face of the man he had been hunting in Tortuga to his present undoing.

The situation was best expressed to Lord Willoughby by van der Kuylen as the pair stepped aboard the Admiral's flag-ship.

"Id is fery boedigal!" he said, his blue eyes twinkling. "Cabdain Blood is fond of boedry—you remember de abble-blossoms. So? Ha, ha!"

—Rafael Sabatini, *Captain Blood*

8 ❀ HERO REDUX

y the time we reach the end of a novel, we
ought to have some very strong feelings about
its hero and heroine. We might love them or
hate them, but we should be involved enough
to care what happens to them. In fact, if the
main character has really lived for us, we may be extremely
reluctant to let go of him, and read with increasing regret as
the end of the book approaches.

If we as readers feel such empathy for a character, imagine
what a novelist faces when he must say good-bye to a creation with whom he has awakened, eaten, slept, drunk,
laughed, cried, and dreamed for months or even years. When
the character is based entirely or even partially on an actual
person, which is often the case, ending the book may mean
ending a remembered or imagined relationship with that
person, as the author relives the encounter as it happened or

rewrites it the way he or she wishes it had happened. But even if the character has come solely from the novelist's imagination, the parting is bittersweet.

So the novelist, bidding good-bye to a hero, may give us one last look, one final image to hold in our memory like a beloved face at the window of a departing train. If it is successful, this last image of the hero or heroine will stay with us long after we close the book. Here is how Kathleen Winsor said good-bye to the heroine of *Forever Amber*: "Amber had picked up her skirts and started to run. Outdoors it was growing light and the sun streaked over the tops of the brick buildings. Her coach stood waiting. As he saw her coming the footman flung open the door and reared back in rigid attention; she laughed and gave a snip of her fingers at his braid-covered chest as she climbed in. Imperturbably he slammed the door, motioned to the driver and the coach rolled forward. Still laughing, she leaned out, and waved at the closed empty windows."

Goodnight, Sweet Princess ✍
The author bids his creation good-bye.

Oh, Carrie, Carrie! Oh, blind strivings of the human heart! Onward, onward, it saith, and where beauty leads, there it follows. Whether it be the tinkle of a lone sheep bell o'er some quiet landscape, or the glimmer of beauty in sylvan places, or the show of soul in some passing eye, the heart knows and makes answer, following. It is when the feet

weary and hope seems vain that the heartaches and the long-
ings arise. Know, then, that for you is neither surfeit nor
content. In your rocking-chair, by your window dreaming,
shall you long, alone. In your rocking-chair, by your window, shall you dream such happiness as you may never feel.

—THEODORE DREISER, *Sister Carrie*

(Marlow completes his telling of the story of Lord Jim.)
"But we can see him, an obscure conqueror of fame, tearing
himself out of the arms of a jealous love at the sign, at the
call of his exalted egoism. He goes away from a living
woman to celebrate his pitiless wedding with a shadowy ideal
of conduct. Is he satisfied—quite, now, I wonder? We ought
to know. He is one of us—and have I not stood up once, like
an evoked ghost, to answer for his eternal constancy? Was I
so very wrong after all? Now he is no more, there are days
when the reality of his existence comes to me with an
immense, with an overwhelming force; and yet upon my
honour there are moments, too, when he passes from my
eyes like a disembodied spirit astray amongst the passions of
this earth, ready to surrender himself faithfully to the claim
of his own world of shades.

"Who knows? He is gone, inscrutable at heart, and the
poor girl is leading a sort of soundless, inert life in Stein's
house. Stein has aged greatly of late. He feels it himself, and
says often that he is 'preparing to leave all this; preparing to
leave . . . ' while he waves his hand sadly at his butterflies."

—JOSEPH CONRAD, *Lord Jim*

So said Hester Prynne, and glanced her sad eyes downward at the scarlet letter. And, after many, many years, a new grave was delved, near an old and sunken one, in that burial-ground beside which King's Chapel has since been built. It was near that old and sunken grave, yet with a space between, as if the dust of the two sleepers had no right to mingle. Yet one tombstone served for both. All around, there were monuments carved with armorial bearings; and on this simple slab of slate—as the curious investigator may still discern, and perplex himself with the purport—there appeared the semblance of an engraved escutcheon. It bore a device, a herald's wording of which might serve for a motto and brief description of our now concluded legend; so sombre is it, and relieved only by one everglowing point of light gloomier than the shadow:—

"ON A FIELD, SABLE, THE LETTER A, GULES."

—NATHANIEL HAWTHORNE, *The Scarlet Letter*

The hoist swung like a pendulum above the city. It sped against the side of the building. It had passed the line where the masonry ended behind her. There was nothing behind her now but steel ligaments and space. She felt the height pressing against her eardrums. The sun filled her eyes. The air beat against her raised chin.

She saw him standing above her, on the top platform of the Wynand Building. He waved to her.

The line of the ocean cut the sky. The ocean mounted as

the city descended. She passed the pinnacles of bank build-ings. She passed the crowns of courthouses. She rose above the spires of churches.

Then there was only the ocean and the sky and the figure of Howard Roark.

—AYN RAND, *The Fountainhead*

(Temple Drake, rescued from a Memphis brothel, her mind unstable, is taken by her father to live in Paris.)
In the pavilion a band in the horizon blue of the army played Massenet and Scriabine, and Berlioz like a thin coating of tortured Tschaikovsky on a slice of stale bread, while the twilight dissolved in wet gleams from the branches, onto the pavilion and the sombre toadstools of umbrellas. Rich and resonant the brasses crashed and died in the thick green twi-light, rolling over them in rich sad waves. Temple yawned behind her hand, then she took out a compact and opened it upon a face in miniature sullen and discontented and sad. Beside her her father sat, his hands crossed on the head of his stick, the rigid bar of his moustache beaded with moisture like frosted silver. She closed the compact and from beneath her smart new hat she seemed to follow with her eyes the waves of music, to dissolve into the dying brasses, across the pool and the opposite semicircle of trees where at sombre intervals the dead tranquil queens in stained marble mused, and on into the sky lying prone and vanquished in the embrace of the season of rain and death.

—WILLIAM FAULKNER, *Sanctuary*

Detail of the last page of the original manuscript of William Faulkner's *Sanctuary*. (*William Faulkner Collections, Manuscripts Division, Special Collections Department, University of Virginia Library*)

(Clarissa Dalloway married Richard Dalloway, an MP, instead of Peter Walsh, who has returned to London after five years in India.)
"Richard has improved. You are right," said Sally. "I shall go and talk to him. I shall say good-night. What does the brain matter," said Lady Rosseter, getting up, "compared with the heart?"

"I will come," said Peter, but he sat on for a moment. What is this terror? what is this ecstasy? he thought to himself. What is it that fills me with extraordinary excitement?

It is Clarissa, he said.

For there she was.

—VIRGINIA WOOLF, *Mrs. Dalloway*

(Dick Diver, the psychiatrist who has treated and married Nicole Warren, living a rich life on the Riviera, returns to America after their divorce.)
After that he didn't ask for the children to be sent to America and didn't answer when Nicole wrote asking him if he needed money. In the last letter she had from him he told her that he was practising in Geneva, New York, and she got the impression that he had settled down with someone to keep house for him. She looked up Geneva in an atlas and found it was in the heart of the Finger Lakes section and considered a pleasant place. Perhaps, so she liked to think, his career was biding its time, again like Grant's in Galena; his latest note was post-marked from Hornell, New York, which is some distance from Geneva and a very small town; in any case he is almost certainly in that section of the country, in one town or other.

—F. SCOTT FITZGERALD, *Tender Is the Night*

Thus Velvet was not fifteen when the thing left her and passed on, the alienating substance, the glory-wine. She was like a child who is offered wine too young and does not really drink. She put her lips to the goblet while thinking of other things. She got off. She glanced the most acute and heady danger and got off. The Press blew, the public stared, hands flew out like a million little fishes after bread. Velvet had shone, a wonder, a glory, a miracle child.

And now, finished with that puzzling mixture of insane intimacy and isolation which is notoriety, Velvet was able to get on quietly to her next adventures. For obviously she was a person to whom things happened, since in a year she had become an heiress, got a horse for a shilling, and won the Grand National.

—ENID BAGNOLD, *National Velvet*

(Humbert Humbert has murdered Clare Quilty for running off with his child lover, Lolita, who marries Richard F. Schiller, and dies in childbirth.)

. . . I wish this memoir to be published only when Lolita is no longer alive.

Thus, neither of us is alive when the reader opens this book. But while the blood still throbs through my writing hand, you are still as much part of blessed matter as I am, and I can still talk to you from here to Alaska. Be true to your Dick. Do not let other fellows touch you. Do not talk to strangers. I hope you will love your baby. I hope it will be a boy. That husband of yours, I hope, will always treat you well, because otherwise my specter shall come at him, like black smoke, like a demented giant, and pull him apart nerve by nerve. And do not pity C.Q. One had to choose between him and H.H., and one wanted H.H. to exist at least a couple of months longer, so as to have him make you live in the minds of later generations. I am thinking of aurochs and angels, the secret of durable pigments, prophetic sonnets, the refuge of art. And this is the only immortality you and I may share, my Lolita.

—VLADIMIR NABOKOV, *Lolita*

This was the road over which Ántonia and I came on that night when we got off the train at Black Hawk and were bedded down in the straw, wondering children, being taken we knew not whither. I had only to close my eyes to hear the rumbling of the wagons in the dark, and to be again overcome by that obliterating strangeness. The feelings of that night were so near that I could reach out and touch them with my hand. I had the sense of coming home to myself, and of having found out what a little circle man's experience is. For Ántonia and for me, this had been the road of Destiny; had taken us to those early accidents of fortune which predetermined for us all that we can ever be. Now I understood that the same road was to bring us together again. Whatever we had missed, we possessed together the precious, the incommunicable past.

—WILLA CATHER, *My Ántonia*

(The Duke of Avon takes a girl from the gutter, proves that she is an aristocrat by birth and marries her.)
His Grace was at her side, and lifted her down from the chair.

"My infant," he said, "duchesses do not dance on chairs, nor do they call their brothers *imbécile*."

Léonie twinkled irrepressibly.

"I do," she said firmly.

Rupert shook his head at her.

"Justin's in the right of it," he said. "You'll have to mend your ways, spitfire. No more bouquets from Princes of the Blood, eh, Justin? Dignity! That's the thing! You must let your hair grow too, and speak to me politely. I'll be pinked an I'll have a sister who tells all my friends I'm an imbecile! Politeness, my lady, and some of your husband's haughtiness! That's what you must have, isn't it, Fan?"

"Ah, bah!" said the Duchess of Avon.

—GEORGETTE HEYER, *These Old Shades*

Will the waves one day carry to him this manuscript containing the history of his life? Shall I ever know the name of this man? Will the missing vessel tell us by its nationality that of Captain Nemo?

I hope so. And I also hope that his powerful vessel has conquered the sea at its most terrible gulf, and that the *Nautilus* has survived where so many other vessels have been lost! If it be so—if Captain Nemo still inhabits the ocean, his adopted country, may hatred be appeased in that savage heart! May the contemplation of so many wonders extinguish for ever the spirit of vengeance! May the judge disappear, and the philosopher continue the peaceful exploration of the sea! If his destiny be strange, it is also sublime. Have I not understood it myself? Have I not lived ten months of this unnatural life? And to the question asked by Ecclesiastes 3000 years ago, "That which is far off and exceeding deep, who can find it out?" two men alone of all now living have the right to give an answer—

CAPTAIN NEMO AND MYSELF.

  —JULES VERNE, *Twenty Thousand Leagues Under the Sea*,
    standard trans. attributed to Mercier Lewis

Of Silver we have heard no more. That formidable seafaring man with one leg has at last gone clean out of my life; but I dare say he met his old Negress, and perhaps still lives in comfort with her and Captain Flint. It is to be hoped so, I suppose, for his chances for comfort in another world are very small.

The bar silver and the arms still lie, for all that I know, where Flint buried them; and certainly they shall lie there for me. Oxen and wain-ropes would not bring me back again to that accursed island; and the worst dreams that ever I have are when I hear the surf booming about its coasts, or start upright in bed, with the sharp voice of Captain Flint still ringing in my ears: "Pieces of eight! pieces of eight!"

  —ROBERT LOUIS STEVENSON, *Treasure Island*

As long as Lady Lyndon lived, Barry enjoyed his income, and was perhaps as happy in prison as at any period of his existence; when her ladyship died, her successor sternly cut off the annuity, devoting the sum to charities: which, he said, would make a nobler use of it than the scoundrel who had enjoyed it hitherto. At his lordship's death, in the Spanish campaign, in the year 1811, his estate fell in to the family of the Tiptoffs, and his title merged in their superior rank; but it does not appear that the Marquis of Tiptoff (Lord George succeeded to the title on the demise of his brother) renewed either the pension of Mr. Barry or the charities which the late lord had endowed. The estate has vastly improved under his lordship's careful management. The trees in Hackton Park are all about forty years old, and the Irish property is rented in exceedingly small farms to the peasantry; who still entertain the stranger with stories of the daring, and the devilry, and the wickedness and the fall of Barry Lyndon.

—WILLIAM MAKEPEACE THACKERAY,
The Memoirs of Barry Lyndon, Esquire

Auntie Mame took Mike by the hand and looked lovingly into his eyes. "Tell me, my little love, do you like the school you go to?"

"No, I don't," Mike said.

"There's such an interesting man here from Madras. He has a whole new conception of education, Michael. It's an interracial school for boys and girls of all nations and colors. It's held in the out-of-doors, and instead of books . . . "

"I said I wanted him back *before* Labor Day!" I sputtered.

"This man is right here at the party now, my little love," she said to Mike, "and I'm sure he'd like to meet you. Come along with me and we'll find him. Enjoy yourselves, darlings," she said over her shoulder.

"My God," Pegeen gasped, "she's the Pied Piper."

Holding Mike's hand, Auntie Mame drifted into the crowd, her sari floating out behind her.

—PATRICK DENNIS, *Auntie Mame*

(Bertie Wooster is determined to fire his valet, Jeeves, for saving the day for a friend of Bertie's by intimating that his employer was "a looney.")

And then through the doorway there shimmered good old Jeeves in the wake of a tray full of the necessary ingredients, and there was something about the mere look of the man. . . .

However, I steeled the old heart and had a stab at it.

"I have just met Mr. Little, Jeeves," I said.

"Indeed, sir?"

"He—er—he told me you had been helping him."

"I did my best, sir. And I am happy to say that matters now appear to be proceeding smoothly. Whisky, sir?"

"Thanks. Er—Jeeves."

"Sir?"

"Another time . . ."

"Sir?"

"Oh, nothing . . . Not all the soda, Jeeves."

"Very good, sir."

He started to drift out.

"Oh, Jeeves!"

"Sir?"

"I wish . . . that is . . . I think . . . I mean . . . Oh, nothing!"

"Very good, sir. The cigarettes are at your elbow, sir. Dinner will be ready at a quarter to eight precisely, unless you desire to dine out?"

"No. I'll dine in."

"Yes, sir."

"Jeeves!"

"Sir?"

"Oh nothing!" I said.

"Very good, sir," said Jeeves.

—P. G. WODEHOUSE, *Jeeves*

9 ❀ THE MASTER THEME

oving insistently beneath the surface of the plot like a tracer line on an oscilloscope, is the theme, the single idea the author wishes to convey. The plot, the series of events that move the story along, may dance wildly up or down, but here and there it touches the theme line, and each time it does it reminds us what the book is really about.

Often the theme is represented by a symbol, like the land in Pearl Buck's *The Good Earth*, or the tree in Betty Smith's *A Tree Grows in Brooklyn*, or the birds in Colleen McCullough's *The Thorn Birds*, and the author will choose to end the book with the strength of that symbol. And so, aged Wang Lung clenches a handful of soil as his sons lie to him, promising they will never sell the land that he has struggled all his life to own. The tree, chopped down until it is only a stump, finds light amid the wash lines in the Brooklyn backyard and begins to grow again. And Meggie, alone and abandoned forever by her priest-lover, realizes she is like the bird that impales itself on a thorn, yet continues to sing until it dies.

The danger of using symbolism is that the novel runs the risk of becoming a treatise instead of a story if the symbolism is overdone. But used well, it crystallizes the theme, melding all the divergent episodes of the book together into a whole. It gives the story a transcendent meaning.

Variation on a Theme ⌒
The central idea of the book is reprised at the end.

A new tree had grown from the stump and its trunk had grown along the ground until it reached a place where there were no wash lines above it. Then it had started to grow towards the sky again.

Annie, the fir tree, that the Nolans had cherished with waterings and manurings, had long since sickened and died. But this tree in the yard—this tree that men chopped down . . . this tree that they built a bonfire around, trying to burn up its stump—this tree lived!

It lived! And nothing could destroy it.

Once more she looked at Florry Wendy reading on the fire escape.

"Goodbye, Francie," she whispered.

She closed the window.

—BETTY SMITH, *A Tree Grows in Brooklyn*

(The grandson of Stan Parker, who has built a homestead in the bush, wanders away from the house where his grandfather has died and writes a poem of life.)

. . . His poem was growing. It would have the smell of bread, and the rather grey wisdom of youth, and his grandmother's kumquats, and girls with yellow plaits exchanging love-talk behind their hands, and the blood thumping like a drum, and red apples, and a little wisp of white cloud that will swell into a horse and trample the whole sky once it gets the wind inside it.

As his poem mounted in him he could not bear it, or rather, what was still his impotence. And after a bit, not knowing what else to do but scribble on the already scribbled trees, he went back to the house in which his grandfather had died, taking with him his greatness, which was still a secret.

So that in the end there were the trees. The boy walking through them with his head drooping as he increased in stature. Putting out shoots of green thought. So that, in the end, there was no end.

—PATRICK WHITE, *The Tree of Man*

He found himself listening for something. It was the sound of the yearling for which he listened, running around the house or stirring on his moss pallet in the corner of the bedroom. He would never hear him again. He wondered if his mother had thrown dirt over Flag's carcass, or if the buzzards had cleaned it. Flag— He did not believe he should ever again love anything, man or woman or his own child, as he had loved the yearling. He would be lonely all his life. But a man took it for his share and went on.

In the beginning of his sleep, he cried out, "Flag!"

It was not his own voice that called. It was a boy's voice. Somewhere beyond the sink-hole, past the magnolia, under the live oaks, a boy and a yearling ran side by side, and were gone forever.

—MARJORIE KINNAN RAWLINGS, *The Yearling*

"She'll be all right, dear. Look at her! Jove!"

There stood Magnolia Ravenal on the upper deck of the Cotton Blossom Floating Palace Theatre, silhouetted against sunset sky and water—tall, erect, indomitable. Her mouth was smiling but her great eyes were wide and sombre. They gazed, unwinking, across the sunlit waters. One arm was raised in a gesture of farewell.

"Isn't she splendid, Ken!" cried Kim, through her tears. "There's something about her that's eternal and unconquerable—like the River."

A bend in the upper road. A clump of sycamores. The river, the show boat, the straight silent figure were lost to view.

—EDNA FERBER, *Show Boat*

(Meggie Cleary muses on the cycle of Nature and her life, from the window of her home, the Australian sheep station, Drogheda.)
Time for Drogheda to stop. Yes, more than time. Let the cycle renew itself with unknown people. I did it all to

myself, I have no one else to blame. And I cannot regret one single moment of it.

The bird with the thorn in its breast, it follows an immutable law; it is driven by it knows not what to impale itself, and die singing. At the very instant the thorn enters there is no awareness in it of the dying to come; it simply sings and sings until there is not the life left to utter another note. But we, when we put the thorns in our breasts, we know. We understand. And still we do it. Still we do it.

—COLLEEN MCCULLOUGH, *The Thorn Birds*

Rabbit comes to the curb but instead of going to his right and around the block he steps down, with as big a feeling as if this little side-street is a wide river, and crosses. He wants to travel to the next patch of snow. Although this block of brick three-stories is just like the one he left, something in it makes him happy; the steps and window sills seem to twitch and shift in the corner of his eye, alive. This illusion trips him. His hands lift of their own and he feels the wind on his ears even before, his heels hitting heavily on the pavement at first but with an effortless gathering out of a kind of sweet panic growing lighter and quicker and quieter, he runs. Ah: runs. Runs.

—JOHN UPDIKE, *Rabbit, Run*

(The scheming Becky Sharp, widowed, wealthy, and calling herself Lady Crawley, busies herself with good works and is considered "an injured woman.")

. . . Her name is in all the Charity Lists. The Destitute Orange-girl, the Neglected Washerwoman, the Distressed Muffin-man, find in her a fast and generous friend. She is always having stalls at Fancy Fairs for the benefit of these hapless beings. Emmy, her children, and the Colonel, coming to London some time back, found themselves suddenly before her at one of these fairs. She cast down her eyes demurely and smiled as they started away from her; Emmy skurrying off on the arm of George (now grown a dashing young gentleman), and the Colonel seizing up his little Janey, of whom he is fonder than of anything in the world—fonder even than of his "History of the Punjaub."

"Fonder than he is of me," Emmy thinks, with a sigh. But he never said a word to Amelia that was not kind and gentle; or thought of a want of hers that he did not try to gratify.

Ah! *Vanitas Vanitatum!* which of us is happy in this world? Which of us has his desire? or, having it, is satisfied?—come, children, let us shut up the box and the puppets, for our play is played out.

—WILLIAM MAKEPEACE THACKERAY, *Vanity Fair*

And the old man let his scanty tears dry upon his cheeks and they made salty stains there. And he stooped and took up a handful of the soil and he held it and he muttered,

"If you sell the land, it is the end."

And his two sons held him, one on either side, each holding his arm, and he held tight in his hand the warm loose earth. And they soothed him and they said over and over, the elder son and the second son,

"Rest assured, our father, rest assured. The land is not to be sold."

But over the old man's head they looked at each other and smiled.

—PEARL BUCK, *The Good Earth*

. . . And those who lay in their beds there felt that they were within a wall that the Abbess had built for them; within all was light and warmth, and without was the darkness they would not exchange even for a relief from pain and from dying. But even while she was talking, other thoughts were passing in the back of her mind. "Even now," she thought, "almost no one remembers Esteban and Pepita, but myself. Camila alone remembers her Uncle Pio and her son; this woman, her mother. But soon we shall die and all memory of those five will have left the earth, and we ourselves shall be loved for a while and forgotten. But the love will have been enough; all those impulses of love return to the love that made them. Even memory is not necessary for love. There is a land of the living and a land of the dead and the bridge is love, the only survival, the only meaning."

—THORNTON WILDER, *The Bridge of San Luis Rey*

About four miles outside the town the Major said to the driver: "Stop a minute, would you, please?"

The driver stopped the jeep.

"Listen," the Major said. "Do you hear something?"

It was a fine sound on the summer air. The tone was good and it must have been loud to hear it as far as this.

"Just a bell," the driver said. "Must be eleven o'clock."

"Yes," the Major said. He looked over the hills across the sea, and the day was as clear as the sound of the bell itself, but the Major could not see or think very clearly.

"Yes," he said, "eleven o'clock."

—JOHN HERSEY, *A Bell for Adano*

A white pillar of flame streaked up hundreds of feet into the night sky as the tremendous detonation tore the heart out of the great fortress of Navarone. No after-fire of any kind, no dark, billowing clouds of smoke, only that one blinding white column that lit up the entire town for a single instant of time, reached up incredibly till it touched the clouds, vanished as if it had never been. And then, by and by, came the shock waves, the solitary thunderclap of the explosion, staggering even at that distance, and finally the deep-throated rumbling as thousands of tons of rock toppled majestically into the harbour—thousands of tons of rock and the two great guns of Navarone.

The rumbling was still in their ears, the echoes fading away far out across the Ægean, when the clouds parted and the moon broke through, a full moon silvering the darkly-rippling waters to starboard, shining iridescently through the spun phosphorescence of the *Sirdar*'s boiling wake. And dead ahead, bathed in the white moonlight, mysterious, remote, the island of Kheros lay sleeping on the surface of the sea.

—ALISTAIR MACLEAN, *The Guns of Navarone*

Put the guns into our hands and we will use them. Give us the slogans and we will turn them into realities. Sing the battle hymns and we will take them up where you left off. Not one not ten not ten thousand not a million not ten millions not a hundred millions but a billion two billions of us all the people of the world we will have the slogans and we will have the hymns and we will have the guns and we will use them and we will live. Make no mistake of it we will live. We will be alive and we will walk and talk and eat and sing and laugh and feel and love and bear our children in tranquillity in security in decency in peace. You plan the wars you masters of men plan the wars and point the way and we will point the gun.

—DALTON TRUMBO, *Johnny Got His Gun*

. . . One morning Tateh looked out the window of his study and saw the three children sitting on the lawn. Behind them on the sidewalk was a tricycle. They were talking and sunning themselves. His daughter, with dark hair, his towheaded stepson and his legal responsibility, the schwartze child. He suddenly had an idea for a film. A bunch of children who were pals, white black, fat thin, rich poor, all kinds, mischievous little urchins who would have funny adventures in their own neighborhood, a society of ragamuffins, like all of us, a gang, getting into trouble and getting out again. Actually not one movie but several were made of this vision. And by that time the era of Ragtime had run out, with the heavy breath of the machine, as if history were no more than a tune on a player piano. We had fought and won the war. The anarchist Emma Goldman had been deported. The beautiful and passionate Evelyn Nesbit had lost her looks and fallen into obscurity. And Harry K. Thaw, having obtained his release from the insane asylum, marched annually at Newport in the Armistice Day parade.

—E. L. DOCTOROW, *Ragtime*

Anyway I bet Im the frist dumb persen in the world who found out some thing inportent for sience. I did somthing but I dont remembir what. So I gess its like I did it for all the dumb pepul like me in Warren and all over the world.

Goodby Miss Kinnian and dr Strauss and evrybody . . .

P.S. please tel prof Nemur not to be such a grouch when pepul laff at him and he woud have more frends. Its easy to have frends if you let pepul laff at you. Im going to have lots of frends where I go.

P.S. please if you get a chanse put some flowrs on Algernons grave in the bak yard.

—DANIEL KEYES, *Flowers for Algernon*

(Retired British Colonel "Tusker" Smalley has died, leaving his wife Lucy to "stay on" in India alone.)

All I'm asking, Tusker, is did you mean it when you said I'd been a good woman to you? And if so, why did you leave me? Why did you leave me here? I am frightened to be alone, Tusker, although I know it is wrong and weak to be frightened—

—but now, until the end, I shall be alone, whatever I am doing, here as I feared, amid the alien corn, waking, sleeping, alone for ever and ever and I cannot bear it but mustn't cry and must must get over it but don't for the moment see how, so with my eyes shut, Tusker, I hold out my hand, and beg you, Tusker, beg, beg you to take it and take me with you. How can you not, Tusker? Oh, Tusker, Tusker, Tusker, how can you make me stay here by myself while you yourself go home?

—PAUL SCOTT, *Staying On*

Dear Fox, old friend, thus we have come to the end of the road that we were to go together. My tale is finished—and so farewell.

But before I go, I have just one more thing to tell you:

Something has spoken to me in the night, burning the tapers of the waning year; something has spoken in the night, and told me I shall die, I know not where. Saying:

"To lose the earth you know, for greater knowing; to lose the life you have, for greater life; to leave the friends you loved, for greater loving; to find a land more kind than home, more large than earth—

"—Whereon the pillars of this earth are founded, toward which the conscience of the world is tending—a wind is rising, and the rivers flow."

—THOMAS WOLFE, *You Can't Go Home Again*

I went up to my room, all attention. The music was over, and I was sorry to have missed the end. I caught an unexpected glimpse of my face in the mirror, and saw myself smile. I didn't try to prevent it; besides, I couldn't have if I'd tried. Once more, and I knew it, I was alone. Alone. Alone. Well, what did it matter? I was a woman who had loved a man. It was a simple story.

—FRANÇOISE SAGAN, *A Certain Smile,*
trans. Anne Green

10 ❀ ONCE UPON A TITLE

ew things are more mysterious or fascinating than the creative process. Where does an idea come from? How does it develop along the lines it does? Why does the author make the choices he or she makes? In the business world, "facilitators" lead brainstorming sessions that attempt to imitate the way the creative mind works. Significantly, although they begin with a stated objective, for example, to find a name for a new product, their method is not to focus on that problem, but to encourage the mind to roam freely. Thus they might ask participants for words to describe the sea, in the case of a shaving lotion, or a barbecue, in the case of a new fast food, and then cull from those free associations combinations of words that suggest themselves as names. The success of these sessions in broadening thinking was considered innovative, but the process is the same the creative mind uses subconsciously. It is: taking the mind by surprise.

The process can easily be observed in the author's choice of a title.

Sometimes the title will be the first thing that comes to the writer, even before a word has been written. But just as often it will be the last, changing and evolving throughout the writing itself, and appearing as an entry on a list of lesser possibilities. Thus *Lady Chatterley's Lover* began as *My Lady's Keeper*; *The Age of Innocence* as *Old New York*; *The Sun Also Rises* variously as *Fiesta, The Last Generation, River to the Sea, Two Lie Together,* and *The Old Leaven;* and *Gone with the Wind* as *The Road to Tara, Another Day, Tomorrow Is Another Day, Tomorrow and Tomorrow, There's Always Tomorrow,* and *Tomorrow Will Be Fair.*

The mind free-associates, but there is a single objective: the title must epitomize the author's theme. It must indicate, to the author at least, what the book is about. Thus we have illustrative titles like *Rabbit Is Rich, Brideshead Revisited, Catch-22, Pride and Prejudice, Vanity Fair,* and *Under the Volcano.* Sometimes the meaning of the title is clear to the reader from the beginning of the book. But often this revelation is saved for the last page, even the last sentence. There it has the effect of bringing the book full circle. We began with the title, wondering what it meant, and we end with the title, its meaning now clear to us.

The Name of the Game ✍

The novel ends with the title.

He fell in October, 1918, on a day that was so quiet and still
on the whole front, that the army report confined itself to
the single sentence: All quiet on the Western Front.

He had fallen forward and lay on the earth as though
sleeping. Turning him over one saw that he could not have
suffered long; his face had an expression of calm, as though
almost glad the end had come.

> —ERICH MARIA REMARQUE,
> *All Quiet on the Western Front,*
> trans. A. W. Wheen

*(Linford, a new boy, has visited the beloved master, Chips, at
Brookfield School before his death.)*
And soon Chips was asleep.

He seemed so peaceful that they did not disturb him to say
good-night; but in the morning, as the School bell sounded
for breakfast, Brookfield had the news. "Brookfield will
never forget his lovableness," said Cartwright, in a speech to
the School. Which was absurd, because all things are forgotten in the end. But Linford, at any rate, will remember and
tell the tale: "I said good-bye to Chips the night before he
died. . . ."

> —JAMES HILTON, *Good-bye, Mr. Chips*

(Sandy, who as a schoolgirl had informed on her eccentric teacher, Miss Brodie, has become Sister Helena of the Transfiguration.)
Monica came again. "Before she died," she said, "Miss Brodie thought it was you who betrayed her."

"It's only possible to betray where loyalty is due," said Sandy.

"Well, wasn't it due to Miss Brodie?"

"Only up to a point," said Sandy.

And there was that day when the enquiring young man came to see Sandy because of her strange book of psychology, "The Transfiguration of the Commonplace," which had brought so many visitors that Sandy clutched the bars of her grille more desperately than ever.

"What were the main influences of your school days, Sister Helena? Were they literary or political or personal? Was it Calvinism?"

Sandy said: "There was a Miss Jean Brodie in her prime."
—MURIEL SPARK, *The Prime of Miss Jean Brodie*

(Elinor Eastlake, driving Harald Petersen to the funeral of his wife, Kay, on whom he had cheated many times, has her revenge by allowing him to think that she, an avowed lesbian, has slept with Kay.)
. . . "You're a coward," Harald said, "to spread your slime on a dead girl. No wonder you hid yourself abroad all those years. You ought to have stayed in Europe, where the lights are going out. You belong there; you're dead. You've never used your mind except to acquire sterile knowledge. You're a

museum parasite. You have no part of America! Let me out!"
"You want to get out of the car?" said Lakey. "Yes," said
Harald. "You bury her. You and the 'group.' " Lakey stopped
the car. He got out. She drove on, following the cortege,
watching him in the rear-view mirror as he crossed the road
and stood, thumbing a ride, while cars full of returning
mourners glided past him, back to New York.

—MARY McCARTHY, *The Group*

Now Sammy's career meteored through my mind in all its
destructive brilliance, his blitzkrieg against his fellow men.
My mind skipped from conquest to conquest, like the scrap-
book on his exploits I had been keeping ever since that
memorable birthday party at the Algonquin. It was a terrify-
ing and wonderful document, the record of where Sammy
ran, and if you looked behind the picture and between the
lines you might even discover what made him run. And
some day I would like to see it published, as a blueprint of a
way of life that was paying dividends in America in the first
half of the twentieth century.

—BUDD SCHULBERG, *What Makes Sammy Run?*

Chingachgook grasped the hand that, in the warmth of feeling, the scout had stretched across the fresh earth, and in that
attitude of friendship these two sturdy and intrepid woodsmen
bowed their heads together, while scalding tears fell to their
feet, watering the grave of Uncas like drops of falling rain.

In the midst of the awful stillness with which such a burst of feeling, coming, as it did, from the two most renowned warriors of that region, was received, Tamenund lifted his voice to disperse the multitude.

"It is enough," he said. "Go, children of the Lenape, the anger of the Manitou is not done. Why should Tamenund stay? The pale-faces are masters of the earth, and the time of the redmen has not yet come again. My day has been too long. In the morning I saw the sons of Unamis happy and strong; and yet, before the night has come, have I lived to see the last warrior of the wise race of the Mohicans."

—JAMES FENIMORE COOPER, *The Last of the Mohicans*

. . . From all across the hot distances of the plain there was no breath of sound. In the small bare room with its bamboo-shaded windows there was no glitter of sun. He picked up the stem of the frangipani flower and held it in his hands. The flowers were still blooming, as the girl had said they would be, with rosy half-opened buds of blossom, and he remembered now that they stood for immortality.

Breathing in the scent of them in a great gasp that was like an agony of relief and pleasure, he lay with his body against her and shut his eyes. Her body felt young and trembling with the breath of sleep and now there was nothing more he asked for but to lie beside it and sleep too.

Outside, the plain was purple in the falling dusk, and the long day was over.

—H. E. BATES, *The Purple Plain*

Then one day at a friend's house I met a cousin of hers and liked him and he liked me. For a week I went out with him constantly, and my father, who could not bear to be alone, followed my example with a rather ambitious young woman. Life began to take its old course, as it was bound to. Now, when my father and I are alone together, we joke and discuss our latest conquests. He must suspect that my friendship with Philippe is not platonic, and I know very well that his new friend is costing him too much money. But we are happy. Winter is drawing to an end. We shall not rent the same villa again, but another one, near Juan-les-Pins.

Only when I am in bed, at dawn, listening to the cars passing below in the streets of Paris, my memory betrays me. That summer returns to me with all its memories. Anne, Anne, I repeat over and over again softly in the darkness. Something rises in me that I call to by name, with closed eyes. *Bonjour, tristesse!*

—FRANÇOISE SAGAN, *Bonjour Tristesse,*
trans. Irene Ash

Maule's well, all this time, though left in solitude, was throwing up a succession of kaleidoscopic pictures, in which a gifted eye might have seen foreshadowed the coming fortunes of Hepzibah and Clifford, and the descendant of the legendary wizard, and the village maiden, over whom he had thrown Love's web of sorcery. The Pyncheon Elm, moreover, with what foliage the September gale had spared to it, whispered unintelligible prophecies. And wise Uncle Venner, passing slowly from the ruinous porch, seemed to hear a strain of music, and fancied that sweet Alice Pyncheon—after witnessing these deeds, this bygone woe and this present happiness, of her kindred mortals— had given one farewell touch of a spirit's joy upon her harpsichord, as she floated heavenward from the HOUSE OF THE SEVEN GABLES!

    —NATHANIEL HAWTHORNE, *The House of the Seven Gables*

Still the towers of Trebizond, the fabled city, shimmer on a far horizon, gated and walled and held in a luminous enchantment. It seems that for me, and however much I must stand outside them, this must for ever be. But at the city's heart lie the pattern and the hard core, and these I can never make my own: they are far outside my range. The pattern should perhaps be easier, the core less hard.

    This, indeed, seems the eternal dilemma.

    —ROSE MACAULAY, *The Towers of Trebizond*

The following day the body of a man was buried in an unmarked grave at Père Lachaise cemetery in Paris. The death certificate showed the body to be that of an unnamed foreign tourist, killed on Sunday August 25, 1963, in a hit-and-run accident on the motorway outside the city. Present were a priest, a policeman, a registrar, and two gravediggers. Nobody present showed any interest as the plain deal coffin was lowered into the grave, except the single other person who attended. When it was all over he turned round, declined to give his name, and walked back down the cemetery path, a solitary little figure, to return home to his wife and children.

The day of the Jackal was over.

—FREDERICK FORSYTH, *The Day of the Jackal*

(After the death of his son, Aureliano locks himself in his room to read a one-hundred-year-old manuscript by Melquíades describing his destiny and the destruction of the hamlet, Macondo.)

. . . Macondo was already a fearful whirlwind of dust and rubble being spun about by the wrath of the biblical hurricane when Aureliano skipped eleven pages so as not to lose time with facts he knew only too well, and he began to decipher the instant that he was living, deciphering it as he lived it, prophesying himself in the act of deciphering the last page of the parchments, as if he were looking into a speaking mirror. Then he skipped again to anticipate the predictions and ascertain the date and circumstances of his death. Before reaching the final line, however, he had already understood that he would never leave that room, for it was foreseen that the city of mirrors (or mirages) would be wiped out by the wind and exiled from the memory of men at the precise moment when Aureliano Babilonia would finish deciphering the parchments, and that everything written on them was unrepeatable since time immemorial and forever more, because races condemned to one hundred years of solitude did not have a second opportunity on earth.

—GABRIEL GARCÍA MÁRQUEZ,
One Hundred Years of Solitude,
trans. Gregory Rabassa

(Huw Morgan remembers his Welsh home and the minister who inspired him to leave it.)
Is Mr. Gruffydd dead, him, that one of rock and flame, who was friend and mentor, who gave me his watch that was all in the world he had, because he loved me? Is he dead, and the tears still wet on my face and my voice cutting through rocks in my throats for minutes while I tried to say goodbye, and, O God, the words were shy to come, and I went from him wordless, in tears and with blood.

Is he dead?

For if he is, then I am dead, and we are dead, and all of sense a mockery.

How green was my Valley, then, and the Valley of them that have gone.

—RICHARD LLEWELLYN, *How Green Was My Valley*

Down by the stream in back of 124 her footprints come and go, come and go. They are so familiar. Should a child, an adult place his feet in them, they will fit. Take them out and they disappear again as though nobody ever walked there.

By and by all trace is gone, and what is forgotten is not

only the footprints but the water too and what it is down there. The rest is weather. Not the breath of the disremembered and unaccounted for, but wind in the eaves, or spring ice thawing too quickly. Just weather. Certainly no clamor for a kiss.

Beloved.

—TONI MORRISON, *Beloved*

Like other doctors, Jenny Garp took that sacred oath of Hippocrates, the so-called father of medicine, wherein she agreed to devote herself to something like the life Garp once described to young Whitcomb—although Garp was concerned with a *writer's* ambitions (". . . trying to keep everyone alive, forever. Even the ones who must die in the end. They're the most important to keep alive"). Thus, cancer research did not depress Jenny Garp, who liked to describe herself as her father had described a novelist.

"A doctor who sees only terminal cases."

In the world according to her father, Jenny Garp knew, we must have energy. Her famous grandmother, Jenny Fields, once thought of us as Externals, Vital Organs, Absentees, and Goners. But in the world according to Garp, we are all terminal cases.

—JOHN IRVING, *The World According to Garp*

"One thing more," said George, as he stopped the congratulations of the throng; "you all remember our good old Uncle Tom?"

George here gave a short narration of the scene of his death, and of his loving farewell to all on the place, and added,

"It was on his grave, my friends, that I resolved, before God, that I would never own another slave, while it was possible to free him; that nobody, through me, should ever run the risk of being parted from home and friends, and dying on a lonely plantation, as he died. So, when you rejoice in your freedom, think that you owe it to that good old soul, and pay it back in kindness to his wife and children. Think of your freedom, every time you see UNCLE TOM'S CABIN; and let it be a memorial to put you all in mind to follow in his steps, and be as honest and faithful and Christian as he was."

—HARRIET BEECHER STOWE, *Uncle Tom's Cabin*

Of Lorna, of my lifelong darling, of my more and more loved wife, I will not talk; for it is not seemly, that a man should exalt his pride. Year by year, her beauty grows, with the growth of goodness, kindness, and true happiness— above all with loving. For change, she makes a joke of this, and plays with it, and laughs at it; and then, when my slow nature marvels, back she comes to the earnest thing. And if I wish to pay her out for something very dreadful—as may happen once or twice, when we become too gladsome—I bring her to forgotten sadness, and to me for cure of it, by the two words, "Lorna Doone."

—R. D. BLACKMORE, *Lorna Doone*

(Ayacanora returns to tend the blinded sea captain, Amyas Leigh, who has wronged her.)
From that hour Ayacanora's power of song returned to her; and day by day, year after year, her voice rose up within that happy home, and soared, as on a skylark's wings, into the highest heaven, bearing with it the peaceful thoughts of the blind giant back to the Paradises of the West, in the wake of the heroes who from that time forth sailed out to colonise another and a vaster England, to the heaven-prospered cry of WESTWARD-HO!

—CHARLES KINGSLEY, *Westward Ho!*

And there we must leave them for the moment, leave them looking out of the great palace windows into the blue of Africa, blue as if the blue swell of the Atlantic itself were breaking over the blue of the mountain beyond, because at that moment the light of which Mopani had spoken, the meaning of all that had happened, came to them like the story of a wind from a far-off place, and at last they felt it.

—LAURENS VAN DER POST, *A Far-Off Place*

(Michael Mont lights his pipe and walks in the night air after the death of Soames Forsyte.)

A drift of music came down the river. There would be a party at some house. They were dancing probably, as he had seen the gnats dancing that afternoon! And then something out of the night seemed to catch him by the throat. God! It was beautiful, amazing! Breathing, in this darkness, as many billion shapes as there were stars above, all living, and all different! What a world! The Eternal Mood at work! And if you died, like that old boy, and lay forever beneath a crab-apple tree—well, it was the Mood resting a moment in your still shape—no! not even resting, moving on in the mysterious rhythm that one called Life. Who could arrest the moving Mood—who wanted to? And if some pale possessor like that poor old chap, tried and succeeded for a moment, the stars twinkled just a little more when he was gone. To have and to hold! As though you could!

And Michael drew in his breath. A sound of singing came down the water to him, trailing, distant, high, and sweet. It was as if a swan had sung!

—JOHN GALSWORTHY, *The Forsyte Saga [Swan Song]*

11 ❀ SHEER POETRY

t was a popular practice in the early years of the novel to begin each chapter with a line or verse of poetry that indicated the tenor of the chapter that was to follow. Poetry or scriptural quotations were also popularly used to *end* books, elevating the text to a plane that was necessarily more ethereal than pure prose. Poetry added a symbolic, often ironic, emphasis to a novel's conclusion. Sometimes the verse came like a benediction.

Although beginning chapters with verse is less popular today, ending with verse can hardly be considered outdated when it has been used by contemporary authors as varied as Paul Scott, Thomas Pynchon, Günter Grass, and Leon Uris. If the author is also a poet, the verse that ends the book might even be original. Otherwise it could be a bit of doggerel, a biblical quotation, a nursery rhyme, a song, or a fragment of a prayer.

A Turn for the Verse 〜

Poetry says it all.

Ivanhoe distinguished himself in the service of Richard, and was graced with farther marks of the royal favour. He might have risen still higher, but for the premature death of the heroic Coeur-de-Lion, before the Castle of Chaluz, near Limoges. With the life of a generous, but rash and romantic monarch, perished all the projects which his ambition and his generosity had formed; to whom may be applied, with a slight alteration, the lines composed by Johnson for Charles of Sweden—

> His fate was destined to a foreign strand,
> A petty fortress and an "humble" hand;
> He left the name at which the world grew pale,
> To point a moral, or adorn a TALE.
>
> —SIR WALTER SCOTT, *Ivanhoe*

(In a deserted corner of the Potters' field of the cemetery of Père Lachaise in Paris is the grave of Jean Valjean.)
. . . This stone is exempt no more than the rest from the leprosy of time, from the mould, the lichen, and the droppings of the birds. The air turns it black, the water green. It is near no

path, and people do not like to go in that direction, because the grass is high, and they would wet their feet. When there is a little sunshine, the lizards come out. There is, all about, a rustling of wild oats. In the spring, the linnets sing in the tree.

This stone is entirely blank. The only thought in cutting it was of the essentials of the grave, and there was no other care than to make this stone long enough and narrow enough to cover a man.

No name can be read there.

Only many years ago, a hand wrote upon it in pencil these four lines which have become gradually illegible under the rain and the dust, and which are probably effaced:

> *Il dort. Quoique le sort fût pour lui bien étrange,*
> *Il vivait. Il mourut quand il n'eut plus son ange.*
> *La chose simplement d'elle-même arriva,*
> *Comme la nuit se fait lorsque le jour s'en va.**

—VICTOR HUGO, *Les Misérables,*
trans. Charles E. Wilbour

*He sleeps. He lived though fate to him was strange,
His angel left him and he died; the change
Came in a natural and simple way,
As night is made when fades from sight the day.

(trans. M. Jules Gray)

(After Billy Budd's death, a ballad, "Billy in the Darbies," is circulated among the crew.)

. . . Ay, Ay, all is up; and I must up too
Early in the morning, aloft from alow.
On an empty stomach, now, never it would do.
They'll give me a nibble—bit o' biscuit ere I go.
Sure, a messmate will reach me the last parting cup;
But, turning heads away from the hoist and the belay,
Heaven knows who will have the running of me up!
No pipe to those halyards.—But aren't it all sham?
A blur's in my eyes; it is dreaming that I am.
A hatchet to my hawser? all adrift to go?
The drum roll to grog, and Billy never know?
But Donald he has promised to stand by the plank;
So I'll shake a friendly hand ere I sink.
But—no! It is dead then I'll be, come to think.—
I remember Taff the Welshman when he sank.
And his cheek it was like the budding pink.
But me they'll lash me in hammock, drop me deep.
Fathoms down, fathoms down, how I'll dream fast asleep.
I feel it stealing now. Sentry, are you there?
Just ease this darbies at the wrist, and roll me over fair,
I am sleepy, and the oozy weeds about me twist.

—HERMAN MELVILLE, *Billy Budd*

(The mother of Gary Gilmore lives in a trailer camp after his execution.)

. . . She had received letters that threatened her life and she ignored them. Letters could not hurt a woman whose son had taken four bullets through the heart.

She also received letters from people who wrote songs about Gary and wanted her permission to publish. She ignored such letters also.

She would just sit there. If a car came at night, came into the trailer park, drove around and slowed up, if it stopped, she knew somebody out in that car was thinking that she was alone by the window. Then she would say to herself, "If they want to shoot me, I have the same kind of guts Gary has. Let them come."

> *Deep in my dungeon*
> > *I welcome you here*
> *Deep in my dungeon*
> > *I worship your fear*
> *Deep in my dungeon,*
> > *I dwell.*
> *I do not know*
> > *if I wish you well.*
>
> *Deep in my dungeon*
> > *I welcome you here*
> *Deep in my dungeon*
> > *I worship your fear*

Deep in my dungeon,
I dwell.
A bloody kiss
from the wishing well.
—old prison rhyme

—NORMAN MAILER, *The Executioner's Song*

"Danny!" she shouted over the din.

"Kathy. . . Kathy!" And they fought through the mass of hurrying people into each other's arms.

I saw them move to the top of the steps. An older man was there and a boy. Danny took off his cap and reached for the man's hand. I could see his lips move. "Hello, Dad . . . I'm home."

I saw the four of them fade into the shadows of the barn–like station. Danny turned and raised his hand at the door for a moment. "So long, Mac."

And they stepped into the twilight. The rain had stopped.

"Train for Wilmington, Philadelphia, Newark, and New York . . . Gate twenty-two."

I walked down the steps.

"Read all about it! Marines on Iwo Jima!"

"All right, you people! Get aboard!"

And I remembered the words in the book I had taken from Marion's body.

Home is the sailor, home from the sea,
And the hunter, home from the hill. . . .

—LEON M. URIS, *Battle Cry*

(To help his small son understand his heritage, Matthew Hazard has the boy's picture taken with an officer's hat Lincoln had given him as a boy.)

"That's my dandy boy," said the photographer, fixing eternity in the instant. He pressed the bulb. The picture was a success.

Now and then, in later years, when Matthew Hazard looked at it, he knew again something of the feeling that had brought it to be, and this in turn made images and sounds, all brought together for the son whom he hoped to give to the Army, with such a blessing as had been his own, in the possession of the Lincoln cap, and in such a heart for the soldier's life as sounded again in the memory of his commander's voice singing,

> Johnny, did you say goodbye?
>> Oh, yes, father.
> I kissed them one and all goodbye,
> I said now don't you go and cry,
> For I'll be homing by and by,
>> Oh, yes, father.

—PAUL HORGAN, *A Distant Trumpet*

(Francis Majcinek has hanged himself; an inquest report is followed by the poem, "Epitaph: The Man with the Golden Arm.")

. . . For it's all in the wrist with a deck or a cue
And if he crapped out when we thought he was due
It must have been that the dice were rolled,
For he had the touch, and his arm was gold:

Rack up his cue, leave the steerer his hat,
The arm that held up has failed at last.

Yet why does the light down the dealer's slot
Sift soft as light in a troubled dream?
(A dream, they say, of a golden arm
That belonged to the dealer we called Machine.)

—NELSON ALGREN, *The Man with the Golden Arm*

(Guy Perron reflects as the English leave India to independence and
partition, remembering an Indian poem he now knows by heart.)

Everything means something to you; dying flowers,
The different times of year.
The new clothes you wear at the end of Ramadan.
A prince's trust. The way that water flows,
Too impetuous to pause, breaking over
Stones, rushing towards distant objects,
Places you can't see but which you also flow
Outward to.

Today you slept long. When you woke your old blood
stirred.
This too meant something. The girl who woke you
Touched your brow.
She called you Lord. You smiled,
Put up a trembling hand. But she had gone,
As seasons go, as a night-flower closes in the day,
As a hawk flies into the sun or as the cheetah runs; as

The deer pauses, sun-dappled in long grass,
But does not stay.

Fleeting moments: these are held a long time in the eye,
The blind eye of the ageing poet,
So that even you, Gaffur, can imagine
In this darkening landscape
The bowman lovingly choosing his arrow,
The hawk outpacing the cheetah,
(The fountain splashing lazily in the courtyard),
The girl running with the deer.

—PAUL SCOTT, *The Raj Quartet [A Division of the Spoils]*

*(Oskar Matzerath, the dwarf whose voice has the power to break
glass, is condemned for a murder of which he is innocent and put in
a mental hospital.)*
. . . Don't ask Oskar who she is! Words fail me. First she was
behind me, later she kissed my hump, but now, now and forever, she is in front of me, coming closer.

Always somewhere behind me, the Black Witch.
Now ahead of me, too, facing me, Black.
Black words, black coat, black money.
But if children sing, they sing no longer:
Where's the Witch, black as pitch?
Here's the black, wicked Witch.
Ha! ha! ha!

—GÜNTER GRASS, *The Tin Drum,*
trans. Ralph Manheim

And there we will leave them to their useful, humdrum, happy domestic existence—than which there is no better that I know of, at their time of life—and no better time of life than theirs!

*"Où peut-on être mieux qu'au sein de sa famille?"**

That blessed harbor of refuge well within our reach, and having really cut our wisdom teeth at last, and learned the ropes, and left off hankering after the moon—we can do with so little down here. . . .

> A little work, a little play
> To keep us going—and so, good-day!
>
> A little warmth, a little light
> Of love's bestowing—and so, good-night!
>
> A little fun, to match the sorrow
> Of each day's growing—and so, good-morrow!
>
> A little trust that when we die
> We reap our sowing! And so—good-bye!

—GEORGE DU MAURIER, *Trilby*

She is silent, she will never speak, never forgive, never reach a hand, never leave this frozen present tense. All waits, suspended. Suspend the autumn trees, the autumn sky, anony-

---

* *"Where can one feel better than in the bosom of one's family?"*
(trans. John Leich)

mous people. A blackbird, poor fool, sings out of season from the willows by the lake. A flight of pigeons over the houses; fragments of freedom, hazard, an anagram made flesh. And somewhere the stinging smell of burning leaves.

> cras amet qui numquam amavit
> quique amavit cras amet*
>
> —JOHN FOWLES, *The Magus*

And it is just here, just at this dark and silent frame, that the pointed tip of the Rocket, falling nearly a mile per second, absolutely and forever without sound, reaches its last unmeasurable gap above the roof of this old theatre, the last delta-t.

There is time, if you need the comfort, to touch the person next to you, or to reach between your own cold legs . . . or, if song must find you, here's one They never taught anyone to sing, a hymn by William Slothrop, centuries forgotten and out of print, sung to a simple and pleasant air of the period. Follow the bouncing ball:

> There is a Hand to turn the time,
> Though thy Glass today be run,
> Till the Light that hath brought the Towers low
> Find the last poor Pret'rite one . . .

* Tomorrow let him love who never
loved before
Whoever has loved and loves no longer,
let him love tomorrow. (trans. John Leich)

Till the Riders sleep by ev'ry road,
All through our crippl'd Zone,
With a face on ev'ry mountainside,
And a Soul in ev'ry stone. . . .

Now everybody—

—THOMAS PYNCHON, *Gravity's Rainbow*

Not that I have time to think of the poor fellow very much.
Mr. Visconti has not yet made a fortune, and our import-
export business takes more and more of my time. We have
had our ups and downs, and the photographs of what we call
the great party and of our distinguished guests have proved
useful more than once. We own a complete Dakota now, for
our partner was accidentally shot dead by a policeman
because he couldn't make himself understood in Guaraní,
and most of my spare time is spent in learning that language.
Next year, when she is sixteen, I am to marry the daughter
of the chief of customs, a union which has the approval of
Mr. Visconti and her father. There is, of course, a considerable difference in our ages, but she is a gentle and obedient
child, and often in the warm scented evenings we read
Browning together.

God's in his heaven—
All's right with the world!

—GRAHAM GREENE, *Travels with My Aunt*

12 ❄ THE EPILOGUE

hat the prologue is to the beginning of the book, the epilogue is to the end. It can leap years ahead to show how life progressed for the novel's characters as we last saw them, just as the prologue stepped back to give us some of their history before we met them in the first chapter. It can wax philosophic or provide information to illuminate what we have just read. It can permit the author, or faux-author (the novelist masquerading as the "writer" of the book) to express personal feelings about the story just told. It can take the form of an appendix, providing the verbatim report of an inquest, a newspaper story or a personal letter to cast light on an otherwise inconclusive ending. And it can bring a story told as a flashback back into the present.

Like the prologue, the epilogue—or conclusion, or finale, as it is variously called—gives the author the option of having a second ending. Thus the novelist can end the story on a high pitch with some action: a marriage, a rescue or a death, for instance, then conclude with a more introspective chapter. The epilogue frees the author from the confines of the story.

In his novel *The French Lieutenant's Woman*, John Fowles even used the last chapter, which is not called an epilogue but functions as one, to rewrite his happy ending with an unhappy one. Fowles introduced a new character, an "impresario," representing Time or Fowles himself as creator, to turn the clock back a quarter of an hour, so that we might read a different ending from the same moment in time. What is interesting is that both endings are completely plausible, and therefore, acceptable to us, even though our emotions are a bit ragged because of the trick that has been played on us. Was the duplicate ending more than a conscious betrayal of the reader? Did Fowles, himself unable to decide between two equally dramatic and intriguing endings, choose to have them both? Which ending did he prefer? Did he rebel against sentencing his romantically mysterious heroine to the conventional marriage that would have been required by the conventionally "happy" ending? In the last analysis, there is some hope even in the second, "unhappy" version, for as Charles Smithson grieves at the loss of Sarah Woodruff to the household of the Rossettis and life as a "New Woman," he has at least found "an atom of faith in himself" on which to build his life again "upon the unplumb'd, salt, estranging sea."

For Tolstoy, finishing *War and Peace*, a single epilogue was not enough (how could it be?), and so he wrote two: the first, which in typical epilogue style picks up the story eight years after the death of Prince Andrey, recounting the happy domestic lives of Pierre and Natasha and Princess Mary and Nicholas after their marriages; and the second, which expounds on the historian's study of human life, free will and necessity, and the forces behind national movements. Most epilogues are not as intricately conceived as this one, which compares in length and complexity to a Shavian preface, but are simply dramatic codas to the stories that have gone before. As they shed further light on a character or an outcome, they are welcome additions to the story and a vital part of the novel itself.

How Tempus Fugits! ⟿
The epilogue spans the years.

(Roger Byam returns to Tahiti eighteen years after he has been taken back to England and finally acquitted of mutiny, to find that his wife, Tehani, has died and his daughter, also called Tehani, has a child.)

"Tehani," called the man beside me, and I caught my breath as she turned, for she had all her dead mother's beauty, and something of my own mother, as well. "The English captain from Matavai," Tuahu was saying, and she gave me her hand graciously. My granddaughter was staring up at me in wonder, and I turned away blindly.

"We must go on," said Tehani to her uncle. "I promised the child she should see the English boat."

"Aye, go," replied Tuahu.

The moon was bright overhead when I reëmbarked in the pinnace to return to my ship. A chill night breeze came whispering down from the depths of the valley, and suddenly the place was full of ghosts,—shadows of men alive and dead,—my own among them.

—CHARLES NORDHOFF AND JAMES NORMAN HALL,
Epilogue, *Mutiny on the Bounty*

(Two friends sit together in Moscow looking through a book of Yurii Zhivago's writings five or ten years after his death and the disappearance of Lara.)
Although victory had not brought the relief and freedom that were expected at the end of the war, nevertheless the portents of freedom filled the air throughout the postwar period, and they alone defined its historical significance.

To the two old friends, as they sat by the window, it seemed that this freedom of the soul was already there, as if that very evening the future had tangibly moved into the streets below them, that they themselves had entered it and were now part of it. Thinking of this holy city and of the entire earth, of the still-living protagonists of this story, and their children, they were filled with tenderness and peace, and they were enveloped by the unheard music of happiness that flowed all about them and into the distance. And the book they held seemed to confirm and encourage their feeling.

—BORIS PASTERNAK, Epilogue, *Doctor Zhivago,*
trans. Max Hayward and Manya Harari

(His street evangelist mother carries on her life and mission after the execution of her son, Clyde, for murder.)
"Kin' I have a dime, grandma? I wana' go up to the corner and git an ice-cream cone." It was the boy asking.

"Yes, I guess so, Russell. But listen to me. You are to come right back."

"Yes, I will, grandma, sure. You know me."

He took the dime that his Grandmother had extracted from a deep pocket in her dress and ran with it to the ice-cream vendor.

Her darling boy. The light and color of her declining years. She must be kind to him, more liberal with him, not restrain him too much, as maybe, maybe, she had—— She looked affectionately and yet a little vacantly after him as he ran. "For *his* sake."

The small company, minus Russell, entered the yellow, unprepossessing door and disappeared.

—THEODORE DREISER, Souvenir, *An American Tragedy*

(D'Artagnan has taken the commission refused by the musketeers: Porthos, who has left the service to marry a rich widow; Aramis, who has retired to a convent; and Athos, who has retired after inheriting a small property. And the cardinal's informant, the husband of the Queen's faithful servant whom the musketeers had rescued . . .)
M. Bonacieux lived on very quietly, wholly ignorant of what had become of his wife, and caring very little about it. One day he had the imprudence to recall himself to the memory of the cardinal. The cardinal had him informed that he

would provide for him so that he should never want for anything in future. In fact, M. Bonacieux, having left his house at seven o'clock in the evening to go to the Louvre, never appeared again in the Rue des Fossoyeurs; the opinion of those who seemed to be best informed was that he was fed and lodged in some royal castle, at the expense of his generous Eminence.

—ALEXANDRE DUMAS, Epilogue, *The Three Musketeers*

(Randolph Ash talks to the child who he thinks is the niece of Christabel La Motte, but who is actually their daughter, a secret he will never learn.)
She held out the finished plait, which he wound in a fine coil, and put into the back of his watch.

"Tell your aunt," he said, "that you met a poet, who was looking for the Belle Dame Sans Merci, and who met you instead, and who sends her his compliments, and will not disturb her, and is on his way to fresh woods and pastures new."

"I'll try to remember," she said, steadying her crown.

So he kissed her, always matter-of-fact, so as not to frighten her, and went on his way.

And on the way home, she met her brothers, and there was a rough-and-tumble, and the lovely crown was broken, and she forgot the message, which was never delivered.

—A. S. BYATT, Postscript 1868, *Possession*

(Seven years after the death of his father, Prince Andrey comes to his son Nikolinka in a dream, and the boy awakes in terror.)
"My father!" he thought. (Although there were two very good portraits of Prince Andrey in the house, Nikolinka never thought of his father in human form.) "My father has been with me, and has caressed me. He approved of me; he approved of Uncle Pierre. Whatever he might tell me, I would do it. Mucius Scaevola burnt his hand. But why should not the same sort of thing happen in my life? I know they want me to study. And I am going to study. But some day I shall have finished, and then I will act. One thing only I pray God for, that the same sort of thing may happen with me as with Plutarch's men, and I will act in the same way. I will do more. Every one shall know of me, shall love me, and admire me." And all at once Nikolinka felt his breast heaving with sobs, and he burst into tears.

"Are you ill?" he heard Dessalle's voice.

"No," answered Nikolinka, and he lay back on his pillow. "How good and kind he is; I love him!" He thought of Dessalle. "But Uncle Pierre! Oh, what a wonderful man! And my father? Father! Father! Yes, I will do something that even *he* would be content with . . . "

—COUNT LEO TOLSTOY, First Epilogue, *War and Peace*, trans. Constance Garnett

(Eppie is to marry and stay with her adopted father, Silas Marner.)
As the bridal group approached, a hearty cheer was raised in the Rainbow yard; and Ben Winthrop, whose jokes had

retained their acceptable flavour, found it agreeable to turn in there and receive congratulations; not requiring the proposed interval of quiet at the Stone-pits before joining the company.

Eppie had a larger garden than she had ever expected there now; and in other ways there had been alterations at the expense of Mr. Cass, the landlord, to suit Silas's larger family. For he and Eppie had declared that they would rather stay at the Stone-pits than go to any new home. The garden was fenced with stones on two sides, but in front there was an open fence, through which the flowers shone with answering gladness, as the four united people came within sight of them.

"O father," said Eppie, "what a pretty home ours is! I think nobody could be happier than we are."

—GEORGE ELIOT, Conclusion, *Silas Marner*

(Karamazov's youngest son, Alyosha, speaks at the funeral of a schoolboy friend as he prepares to accompany his brother Dmitri, wrongly accused of their father's death, to Siberia.)
"Karamazov," cried Kolya, "can it be true what's taught us in religion, that we shall all rise again from the dead and shall live and see each other again, all, Ilusha too?"

"Certainly we shall all rise again, certainly we shall see each other and shall tell each other with joy and gladness all that has happened!" Alyosha answered, half laughing, half enthusiastic.

"Ah, how splendid it will be!" broke from Kolya.

"Well, now we will finish talking and go to his funeral dinner. Don't be put out at our eating pancakes—it's a very old custom and there's something nice in that!" laughed Alyosha. "Well, let us go! And now we go hand in hand."

"And always so, all our lives hand in hand! Hurrah for Karamazov!" Kolya cried once more rapturously, and once more the boys took up his exclamation:

"Hurrah for Karamazov!"

—FYODOR DOSTOYEVSKY,
Epilogue, *The Brothers Karamazov,*
trans. Constance Garnett

The Epilogue as Appendix ⟋
Some further information makes it all clear.

(Epilogue takes the form of a "transcript of the proceedings of the Twelfth Symposium on Gileadean Studies," held at the University of Denay, Nunavit, on June 25, 2195, reporting "historical notes" on the story just told.)

Did our narrator reach the outside world safely and build a new life for herself? Or was she discovered in her attic hiding place, arrested, sent to the Colonies or to Jezebel's, or even executed? Our document, though in its own way eloquent, is on these subjects mute. We may call Eurydice forth from the world of the dead, but we cannot make her answer; and when we turn to look at her we glimpse her only for a moment, before she slips from our grasp and flees. As all historians know, the past is a great darkness, and filled with echoes. Voices may reach us from it; but what they say to us is imbued with the obscurity of the matrix out of which they come; and, try as we may, we cannot always decipher them precisely in the clearer light of our own day.

Applause.

Are there any questions?
> —MARGARET ATWOOD, Historical Notes on the
> Handmaid's Tale, *The Handmaid's Tale*

This manuscript was found after the fire that destroyed the Twin Elms Nursing Home. In a letter found inside the cover, Miss Caroline Spencer requested the Reverend Thornhill to have it published if possible. This has been done with the permission of her brother, John Spencer.
> —MAY SARTON, Afterword, *As We Are Now*

(The keeper of the inn called The Invisible Man gloats over the secret manuscripts left by that strange creature.)
His brows are knit and his lips move painfully. "Hex, little two up in the air, cross and a fiddle-de-dee. Lord! what a one he was for intellect!"

Presently he relaxes and leans back, and blinks through his smoke across the room at things invisible to other eyes. "Full of secrets," he says. Wonderful secrets!

"Once I get the haul of them—*Lord!*

"I wouldn't do what *he* did; I'd just—well!" He pulls at his pipe.

So he lapses into a dream, the undying wonderful dream of his life. And though Kemp has fished unceasingly, and Adye has questioned closely, no human being save the landlord knows those books are there, with the subtle secret of invisibility and a dozen other strange secrets written therein. And none other will know of them until he dies.

—H. G. WELLS, The Epilogue, *The Invisible Man*

. . . Half an hour from now, when I shall again and forever reindue that hated personality, I know how I shall sit shuddering and weeping in my chair, or continue, with the most strained and fearstruck ecstasy of listening, to pace up and down this room (my last earthly refuge) and give ear to every sound of menace. Will Hyde die upon the scaffold? or will he find courage to release himself at the last moment? God knows; I am careless; this is my true hour of death, and what is to follow concerns another than myself. Here then, as I lay down the pen and proceed to seal up my confession, I bring the life of that unhappy Henry Jekyll to an end.

—ROBERT LOUIS STEVENSON,
Henry Jekyll's Full Statement of the Case,
The Strange Case of Dr. Jekyll and Mr. Hyde

When we got home we were talking of the old time—which we could all look back on without despair, for Godalming and Seward are both happily married. I took the papers from the safe where they had been ever since our return so long ago. We were struck with the fact, that in all the mass of material of which the record is composed, there is hardly one authentic document; nothing but a mass of typewriting, except the later note-books of Mina and Seward and myself, and Van Helsing's memorandum. We could hardly ask any one, even did we wish to, to accept these as proofs of so wild a story. Van Helsing summed it all up as he said, with our boy on his knee:—

"We want no proofs; we ask none to believe us! This boy will some day know what a brave and gallant woman his mother is. Already he knows her sweetness and loving care; later on he will understand how some men so loved her, that they did dare much for her sake."

JONATHAN HARKER.

—BRAM STOKER, Note, *Dracula*

I have prayed over his mortal remains, that God might show him mercy notwithstanding his crimes. Yes, I am sure, quite sure that I prayed beside his body, the other day, when they took it from the spot where they were burying the phonographic records. It was his skeleton. I did not recognize it by the ugliness of the head, for all men are ugly when they have been dead as long as that, but by the plain gold ring which he wore and which Christine Daaé had certainly slipped on his finger, when she came to bury him in accordance with her promise.

The skeleton was lying near the little well, in the place where the Angel of Music first held Christine Daaé fainting in his trembling arms, on the night when he carried her down to the cellars of the Opera house.

And, now, what do they mean to do with that skeleton? Surely they will not bury it in the common grave! . . . I say that the place of the skeleton of the Opera ghost is in the archives of the National Academy of Music. It is no ordinary skeleton.

—GASTON LEROUX, Epilogue, *The Phantom of the Opera*

(Ishmael, the lone survivor, tells of his escape from the sinking whaler, Pequod.*)*

. . . So, floating on the margin of the ensuing scene, and in full sight of it, when the half-spent suction of the sunk ship reached me, I was then, but slowly, drawn towards the closing vortex. When I reached it, it had subsided to a creamy pool. Round and round, then, and ever contracting towards the button-like black bubble at the axis of that slowly wheeling circle, like another Ixion, I did revolve. Till, gaining that vital centre, the black bubble upward burst; and now, liberated by the reason of its cunning spring, and owing to its great buoyancy, rising with great force, the coffin life-buoy shot lengthwise from the sea, fell over, and floated by my side. Buoyed up by that coffin, for almost one whole day and night, I floated on a soft and dirge-like main. The unharming sharks, they glided by as if with padlocks on their mouths; the savage sea-hawks sailed with sheathed beaks. On the second day, a sail drew near, nearer, and picked me up at last. It was with the devious-cruising *Rachel*, that in her retracing search after her missing children, only found another orphan.

—HERMAN MELVILLE, Epilogue, *Moby-Dick*

Flash Forward ⌐

The author or narrator brings us back to the present.

So endeth this chronicle. It being strictly a history of a *boy*, it must stop here; the story could not go much further without becoming the history of a *man*. When one writes a novel about grown people, he knows exactly where to stop—that is, with a marriage; but when he writes of juveniles, he must stop where he best can.

Most of the characters that perform in this book still live, and are prosperous and happy. Some day it may seem worth while to take up the story of the younger ones again and see what sort of men and women they turned out to be; therefore it will be wisest not to reveal any of that part of their lives at present.

—MARK TWAIN, Conclusion,
The Adventures of Tom Sawyer

I go to London and see the busy multitudes in Fleet Street and the Strand, and it comes across my mind that they are but the ghosts of the past, haunting the streets that I have seen silent and wretched, going to and fro, phantasms in a dead city, the mockery of life in a galvanised body. And strange, too, it is to stand on Primrose Hill, as I did but a day before writing this last chapter, to see the great province of houses, dim and blue through the haze of the smoke and mist, vanishing at last into the vague lower sky, to see the people walking to and fro among the flower-beds on the hill, to see the sightseers about the Martian machine that stands there still, to hear the tumult of playing children, and to recall the time when I saw it all bright and clear-cut, hard and silent, under the dawn of that last great day. . . .

And strangest of all is it to hold my wife's hand again, and to think that I have counted her, and that she has counted me, among the dead.

—H. G. WELLS, The Epilogue, *The War of the Worlds*

. . . And, as I said before, a decision has been made. I'm shaking off the old skin and I'll leave it here in the hole. I'm coming out, no less invisible without it, but coming out nevertheless. And I suppose it's damn well time. Even hibernations can be overdone, come to think of it. Perhaps that's my greatest social crime. I've overstayed my hibernation, since there's a possibility that even an invisible man has a socially responsible role to play.

"Ah," I can hear you say, "so it was all a build-up to bore

us with his buggy jiving. He only wanted us to listen to him rave!" But only partially true: Being invisible and without substance, a disembodied voice, as it were, what else could I do? What else but try to tell you what was really happening when your eyes were looking through? And it is this which frightens me:

Who knows but that, on the lower frequencies, I speak for you?

—RALPH ELLISON, Epilogue, *Invisible Man*

(Charles Ryder revisits the chapel at Brideshead and reasons with himself.)
"Something quite remote from anything the builders intended, has come out of their work, and out of the fierce little human tragedy in which I played; something none of us thought about at the time; a small red flame—a beaten-copper lamp of deplorable design relit before the beaten-copper doors of a tabernacle; the flame which the old knights saw from their tombs, which they saw put out; that flame burns again for other soldiers, far from home, farther, in heart, than Acre or Jerusalem. It could not have been lit but for the builders and the tragedians, and there I found it this morning, burning anew among the old stones."

I quickened my pace and reached the hut which served us for our ante-room.

"You're looking unusually cheerful today," said the second-in-command.

—EVELYN WAUGH, Epilogue, *Brideshead Revisited*

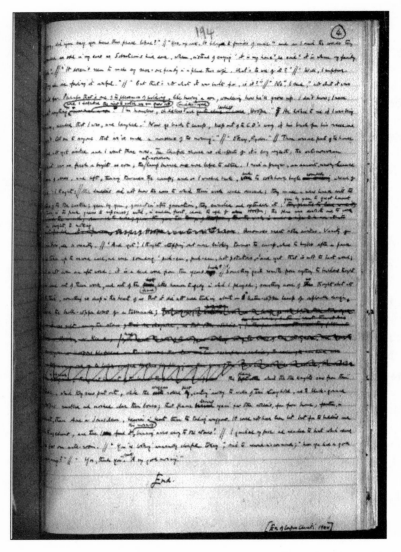

The last page of the original manuscript of Evelyn Waugh's
*Brideshead Revisited. (Harry Ransom Humanities Research Center, The
University of Texas at Austin)*

(Tom Wingo has left his psychiatrist-lover, Susan Lowenstein, to return home to his family.)

Each night, when practice is over and I'm driving home through the streets of Charleston, I ride with the top down on my Volkswagen convertible. It is always dark and the air is crisp with autumn and the wind is rushing through my hair. At the top of the bridge with the stars shining above the harbor, I look to the north and wish again that there were two lives apportioned to every man and woman. Behind me the city of Charleston simmers in the cold elixirs of its own incalculable beauty and before me my wife and children are waiting for me to arrive home. It is in their eyes that I acknowledge my real life, my destiny. But it is the secret life that sustains me now, and as I reach the top of that bridge I say it in a whisper, I say it as a prayer, as regret, and as praise. I can't tell you why I do it or what it means, but each night when I drive toward my southern home and my southern life, I whisper these words: "Lowenstein, Lowenstein."

—PAT CONROY, Epilogue, *The Prince of Tides*

The river of life, of mysterious laws and mysterious choice, flows past a deserted embankment; and along that other deserted embankment Charles now begins to pace, a man behind the invisible gun carriage on which rests his own corpse. He walks towards an imminent, self-given death? I think not; for he has at last found an atom of faith in himself, a true uniqueness, on which to build; has already begun, though he would still bitterly deny it, though there are tears in his eyes to support his denial, to realize that life, however advantageously Sarah may in some ways seem to fit the role of Sphinx, is not a symbol, is not one riddle and one failure to guess it, is not to inhabit one face alone or to be given up after one losing throw of the dice; but is to be, however inadequately, emptily, hopelessly into the city's iron heart, endured. And out again, upon the unplumb'd, salt, estranging sea.

—JOHN FOWLES, Epilogue, *The French Lieutenant's Woman*

. . . A new Theresa will hardly have the opportunity of reforming a conventual life, any more than a new Antigone will spend her heroic piety in daring all for the sake of a brother's burial: the medium in which their ardent deeds took shape is for ever gone. But we insignificant people with our daily words and acts are preparing the lives of many Dorotheas, some of which may present a far sadder sacrifice than that of the Dorothea whose story we know.

Her finely-touched spirit had still its fine issues, though they were not widely visible. Her full nature, like that river of which Cyrus broke the strength, spent itself in channels which had no great name on the earth. But the effect of her being on those around her was incalculably diffusive: for the growing good of the world is partly dependent on unhistoric acts; and that things are not so ill with you and me as they might have been, is half owing to the number who lived faithfully a hidden life, and rest in unvisited tombs.

—GEORGE ELIOT, Finale, *Middlemarch*

(After his sentence and imprisonment in Siberia, with a New Testament given him by Sonia, Raskolnikoff experiences a rebirth.)
. . . He had asked her for it himself not long before his illness and she brought him the book without a word. Till now he had not opened it.

He did not open it now, but one thought passed through his mind: "Can her convictions not be mine now? Her feelings, her aspirations at least. . . ."

She too had been greatly agitated that day, and at night she was taken ill again. But she was so happy—and so unexpectedly happy—that she was almost frightened of her happiness. Seven years, *only* seven years! At the beginning of their happiness at some moments they were both ready to look on those seven years as though they were seven days. He did not know that the new life would not be given him for nothing, that he would have to pay dearly for it, that it would cost him great striving, great suffering.

But that is the beginning of a new story—the story of the gradual renewal of a man, the story of his gradual regeneration, of his passing from one world into another, of his initiation into a new unknown life. That might be the subject of a new story, but our present story is ended.

—FYODOR DOSTOYEVSKY,
Epilogue, *Crime and Punishment,*
trans. Constance Garnett

13 ✽ AUTHOR! AUTHOR!

n *Great Beginnings*, we saw how the author sometimes intruded into the novel, introducing the story as him- or herself or as another, fictional writer, whom we called the faux-author. By this most elemental method of storytelling, the author was able to speak directly to the reader, establishing a feeling of intimacy, and then slowly to withdraw from the story as it took on its own momentum.

Not surprisingly in books where the author has begun as storyteller, the author usually reappears at the end. This allows a certain distancing from the story, so the novelist can comment on it and its characters, express philosophic views, and even contradict what appears to have happened. This last possibility is particularly effective and amusing when the author is pretending to be the discoverer of a journal or other manuscript, and continues the charade by disclaiming personal responsibility for the story.

The reappearance of the author, far from presenting an unsettling intrusion, should renew the pact of confidentiality the author established with the reader at the beginning of the book. The power of this sense of intimacy, of one voice speaking to another, is enormous. It is a phenomenon very unlike the feeling we experience in a theater, where the audience is an active participant and we are one of many. In a book, the author is talking to us alone. It is why we feel that we *know* a writer.

And what could be more remarkable than *knowing* Jane Austen or D. H. Lawrence or Ernest Hemingway!

And Then I Wrote ↩

The author or faux-author puts down his pen.

(". . . if the reader will allow me to seize him affectionately by the arm," writes the author, "we will together take our last farewell of Barset and of the towers of Barchester.")
. . . I may not boast that any beside myself have so realized the place, and the people, and the facts, as to make such reminiscences possible as those which I should attempt to evoke by an appeal to perfect fellowship. But to me Barset has been a real county, and its city a real city, and the spires and towers have been before my eyes, and the voices of the people are known to my ears, and the pavements of the city ways are familiar to my footsteps. To them all I now say

farewell. That I have been induced to wander among them too long by my love of old friendships, and by the sweetness of old faces, is a fault for which I may perhaps be more readily forgiven, when I repeat, with some solemnity of assurance, the promise made in my title, that this shall be the last chronicle of Barset.

—ANTHONY TROLLOPE, *The Last Chronicle of Barset*

As for Davie and Catriona, I shall watch you pretty close in the next days, and see if you are so bold as to be laughing at papa and mamma. It is true we were not so wise as we might have been, and made a great deal of sorrow out of nothing; but you will find as you grow up that even the artful Miss Barbara, and even the valiant Mr. Alan, will be not so very much wiser than their parents. For the life of man upon this world of ours is a funny business. They talk of the angels weeping; but I think they must more often be holding their sides, as they look on; and there was one thing I determined to do when I began this long story, and that was to tell out everything as it befell.

—ROBERT LOUIS STEVENSON, *David Balfour*

Such is my friend's latest development. He would not, it is true, run much chance at present of trying to found a College of Spiritual Pathology, but I must leave the reader to determine whether there is not a strong family likeness between the Ernest of the College of Spiritual Pathology and

the Ernest who will insist on addressing the next generation rather than his own. He says he trusts that there is not, and takes the sacrament duly once a year as a sop to Nemesis lest he should again feel strongly upon any subject. It rather fatigues him, but "no man's opinions," he sometimes says, "can be worth holding unless he knows how to deny them easily and gracefully upon occasion in the cause of charity." In politics he is a Conservative so far as his vote and interest are concerned. In all other respects he is an advanced Radical. His father and grandfather could probably no more understand his state of mind than they could understand Chinese, but those who know him intimately do not know that they wish him greatly different from what he actually is.

—SAMUEL BUTLER, *The Way of All Flesh*

So much I can say: the facts related, with some regretted omissions, by which my story has so skeleton a look, are those that led to the lamentable conclusion. But the melancholy, the pathos of it, the heart of all England stirred by it, have been—and the panting excitement it was to every listener—sacrificed in the vain effort to render events as consequent to your understanding as a piece of logic, through an exposure of character! Character must ever be a mystery, only to be explained in some degree by conduct; and that is very dependent upon accident: and unless we have a perpetual whipping of the tender part of the reader's mind, interest in invisible persons must needs flag. For it is an infant we address, and the story-teller whose art excites an infant to serious attentions succeeds best; with English people assuredly, I rejoice to think, though I pray their patience here while that philosophy and exposure of character block the course along a road inviting to traffic of the most animated kind.

—George Meredith, *The Amazing Marriage*

In spite of the many intricacies of plot and psychology, the story proceeds at a spanking pace. Before we can pause to take breath and quietly survey the new surroundings into which the writer's magic carpet has, as it were, spilled us, another attractive girl, Lucette Veen, Marina's younger daughter, has also been swept off her feet by Van, the irresistible rake. Her tragic destiny constitutes one of the highlights of this delightful book.

The rest of Van's story turns frankly and colorfully upon his long love-affair with Ada. It is interrupted by her marriage to an Arizonian cattle-breeder whose fabulous ancestor discovered our country. After her husband's death our lovers are reunited. They spend their old age traveling together and dwelling in the various villas, one lovelier than another, that Van has erected all over the Western Hemisphere.

Not the least adornment of the chronicle is the delicacy of pictorial detail: a latticed gallery; a painted ceiling; a pretty plaything stranded among the forget-me-nots of a brook; butterflies and butterfly orchids in the margin of the romance; a misty view descried from marble steps; a doe at gaze in the ancestral park; and much, much more.

— VLADIMIR NABOKOV, *Ada or Ardor: A Family Chronicle*

But I must stop rambling. I must cease my everlasting speculations. If I am ever to write anything, even if I give it my whole lifetime, I must still make a beginning. I must still make a mark on the acres of white paper that seem to unroll before me like arctic snows. And I must shut with a man's firmness a journal which seems the softest of self-indulgences in contrast to the austerely empty notebook that now I open.

— LOUIS AUCHINCLOSS, *The Rector of Justin*

(Visiting the equatorial country of Boca Grande, Charlotte Douglas has an affair with the son of Grace Strasser and, refusing to leave with Grace and her son when revolution begins, is wantonly killed.)
When I am tired I remember what I was taught in Colorado. On Day Minus One in Boca Grande Charlotte remembered to bring me a gardenia for my trip. Her mother taught her that. Marin and I are inseparable. She had a straw hat one Easter, and a flowered lawn dress. Tell Charlotte she was wrong. Tell Marin she was wrong. Tell her that for me. She remembers everything. She remembers she bled. The wind is up and I will die and rather soon and all I know empirically is *I am told*.

I am told, and so she said.

I heard later.

According to her passport. It was reported.
Apparently.

I have not been the witness I wanted to be.

        —JOAN DIDION, *A Book of Common Prayer*

And what stories Nell had to tell her parents—of the château and the de Troites, and Eastlake (and the horrible Annabel) and the clouded paradise of Faraway Farm and the puzzling events at Border Kennels. Clifford and Helen were more guarded in what they had to say, as you, reader, will understand. They did not want to hurt each other, or Nell. Besides, the older we grow, the less admirable our pasts must seem.

But how lucky they were, to be given this second chance—and how little, you might think, they deserved it. Our children are to be loved and guarded, not used as pawns in some sad mating-game. And as to whether Helen *should* have taken Clifford back, well, you will have your own opinion. I'm not so sure myself. Not, of course, that Helen would listen to advice. She loved him, as always, and that was that. The best we can do is wish that they all live happily ever after, and I think they have as good a chance as any of actually getting away with it.

        —FAY WELDON, *The Hearts and Lives of Men*

"Get the ship ready, Malluch, and be thou ready to go with me."

"It is well," said Simonides.

"And thou, Esther, what sayest thou?" asked Ben-Hur.

Esther came to his side, and put her hand on his arm, and answered:

"So wilt thou best serve the Christ. O my husband, let me not hinder, but go with thee and help."

* * * * * * * * * *

If any of my readers, visiting Rome, will make the short journey to the Catacomb of San Calixto, which is more ancient than that of San Sebastiano, he will see what became of the fortune of Ben-Hur, and give him thanks. Out of that vast tomb Christianity issued to supersede the Cæsars.

—LEW WALLACE, *Ben-Hur*

And now, as I close my task, subduing my desire to linger yet, these faces fade away. But one face, shining on me like a Heavenly light by which I see all other objects, is above them and beyond them all. And that remains.

I turn my head, and see it, in its beautiful serenity, beside me. My lamp burns low, and I have written far into the night; but the dear presence, without which I were nothing, bears me company.

Oh Agnes, oh my soul, so may thy face be by me when I close my life indeed; so may I, when realities are melting from me like the shadows which I now dismiss, still find thee near me, pointing upward!

—CHARLES DICKENS,
The Personal History of David Copperfield

. . . That is all I can tell of him: I know it is very unsatisfactory; I can't help it. But as I was finishing this book, uneasily conscious that I must leave my reader in the air and seeing no way to avoid it, I looked back with my mind's eye on my long narrative to see if there was any way in which I could devise a more satisfactory ending; and to my intense surprise it dawned upon me that without in the least intending to I had written nothing more nor less than a success story. For all the persons with whom I have been concerned got what they wanted: Elliott social eminence; Isabel an assured position backed by a substantial fortune in an active and cultured community; Gray a steady and lucrative job, with an office to go to from nine till six every day; Suzanne Rouvier security; Sophie death; and Larry happiness. And however superciliously the highbrows carp, we the public in our heart of hearts all like a success story; so perhaps my ending is not so unsatisfactory after all.

—W. SOMERSET MAUGHAM, *The Razor's Edge*

14 ❀ THE END

ife doesn't end. But novels do, and with them the lives and thoughts and dreams we have shared for so short and magical a time. We leave the characters of a book at the zenith of their lives or in the hours of their deaths, and there they remain for us frozen in time. What a weighty responsibility for the author, then, to produce a great ending, one that may grieve or uplift us, but that may also leave us with an indelible memory of the essence and truth of another human being in another time and place.

Just as *Great Beginnings* demonstrated that there is no single right way to begin a book, *Great Endings* shows there are infinite ways to end it, each one unique to its own characters and story and the style of its author. Which is the most successful? Who is to say? Certainly we all have our favorite last images. The green light at the end of the pier in *The Great*

Gatsby. The ravaged fish tied to the boat in *The Old Man and the Sea.*

Why do these endings please us? The answer goes deeper than the beauty of the writing and the satisfaction of an inevitable conclusion. In observing the life and sometimes the death of another being, we ourselves understand more about life and death. Even if the death is a senseless one, we can experience it objectively from a distance. And as we read, we feel a little more secure, having been let in on something of the Great Mystery. Unlike our reactions to real-life tragedy—frustration, anger, fear, helplessness, and bewilderment in the face of victimized goodness and unpunished evil—the end of the novel in its completeness and closure gives us a feeling, however brief, of control, of evil vanquished and righteousness restored.

The novelist is a just and reasonable god.

Author Index

Title Index ∽

Copyright Acknowledgments ✍